ANDREW DEMPSTER has almost 40 years' experience of scrambling and backpacking in the Scottish Highlands and Islands. He has climbed all the Munros twice, and all the Corbetts, and wrote the first guidebook to the Grahams (mountains between 2,000 and 2,500ft in  climbed extensively in such varied locati Africa, Iceland and Greenland. The ever. He is a retired mathematics tea h his wife, Heather, and son, Ruaraid

By the same author:

Classic Mountain Scrambles in Scotland (Mainstream, 1992; Luath, 2016)
The Munro Phenomenon (Mainstream, 1995)
The Grahams (Mainstream, 1997)
Skye 360 (Luath, 2003)
100 Classic Coastal Walks in Scotland (Mainstream, 2011)

The Hughs

Scotland's Best Wee Hills Under 2,000ft

ANDREW DEMPSTER

Luath Press Limited

EDINBURGH

www.luath.co.uk

First published 2015
Reprinted 2017
Reprinted 2018

ISBN: 978-1-910745-03-8

The paper used in this book is recyclable. It is made
from low chlorine pulps produced in a low energy, low emission manner from
renewable forests.

Printed and bound by CPI Antony Rowe, Chippenham.

Typeset in 8.5 point Sabon

Contents

PART 1: SOUTH AND EAST SCOTLAND (50 HUGHS)

Introduction

Meall Lochan a' Chleirich

Introducing the Hughs

THE HUGHS ARE a new category of Scottish hills. All under 2,000ft, they are hills with attitude, not altitude. So what exactly is 'attitude'? The three key words are:

PROMINENCE · POSITION · PANORAMA

I love the Scottish hills and in 40 years of hillwalking (and writing about hillwalking) I have identified a whole host of smaller hills which are rewarding – and often stunning – climbs. The Hughs have been chosen on the basis of this personal experience, rather than on strict quantitative criteria. Their outstanding qualities have inspired me to create this list of the 100 mainland Hughs (a second volume will cover the 100 island Hughs). Some are already popular, many are less well-known. However, I can attest to the fact that there is something very special about each and every one of the Hughs.

This is what the Hughs are about – they are diverse but never dull, small in stature but big in character, charisma and clout – hills small in altitude but big in attitude. I agree with the great fell-walker AW Wainwright when he observed: 'Some misinformed sources have defined a mountain as a hill which exceeds 2,000 feet in height. Of course they are wrong. The status of a mountain is not determined by any arbitrary level of altitude but by appearance. Rocks and ruggedness, roughness of terrain and a commanding presence are the essential qualifications'.

Essential Qualities

Prominence, Position and Panorama are qualities that are not independent of each other: one will influence the other. Let's take two examples. A hill may not be prominent on account of steepness and cragginess, but because it is the highest point for miles around. Similarly, the quality of a hill's summit view is dependent on position. Many Hughs offering marvellous panoramic views, especially in the west and north, are coastal or island hills which benefit from their maritime position.

Arthur's Seat, the most climbed hill in Scotland, possesses all the key attributes of a Hugh. Its prominence ensures that it is the iconic landmark of Edinburgh and its unique position in the centre of Scotland's capital city guarantees an unrivalled panorama, not only of the city, but of the Pentland Hills and the Firth of Forth. Arthur's Seat has attitude.

Another iconic Hugh is the Trossach's little gem, Ben A'n. The character of this hill lies not only in its rocky profile, but also in its position at the centre of the Trossachs, one of Scotland's most scenic areas. There are outstanding views from its craggy, airy summit. Among Hughs blessed with both a fantastic position and wide-ranging summit views (but rarely climbed) is Ben Hutig in the far north (Route 88).

Accessibility

Someone once commented that hills under 2,000 feet are for people over 60. This is unwarranted, given that older folk, some into their 80s, are still capable of climbing Munros. It is true to say that a good number of Hughs are entry-level hills, but some require as much effort and commitment as a Munro or Corbett, especially hills such as Creag Riabhach or the Stack of Glencoul which are situated in remote, wild areas.

Many mainland Hughs are situated in areas mostly devoid of Munros, Corbetts and Grahams – a quarter in the Southern Uplands and the East of Scotland, another quarter straddling the Highland Edge or in the Central Belt. Hughs in settings not characterised by high mountains, such as Meikle Bin in the Campsies and West Lomond in Fife, therefore tend to stand out significantly.

Views

Climbing wee hills and enjoying the view is better than climbing big hills in mist. Big isn't always beautiful. The view from a smaller hill often has impact and three-dimensionality, as it is not looking down on other hills and is less dominated by the horizon.

Probably the best view of the Cuillin ridge on Skye is from a wee hill called Sgurr na Stri. From this island Hugh, there is an unparalleled vista of the entire ridge, of Blaven and of the islands of Soay, Rum and Eigg. I have climbed this rocky eminence on countless occasions, by a variety of routes and never tire of its magic and charm.

Hughs vs Marilyns and Humps

As the *best* hills under 2,000ft, the Hughs do not constitute a comprehensive and all-inclusive list. For that, you must turn to the Marilyns (see Note on Classifications), or extend the Marilyn 150m drop criterion down to 100m and climb what are known as the 'Humps' – a loose acronym of 'Hills with 100m of prominence'. (There are over 1,200 Humps under 2,000ft in Scotland – a list too far in my opinion. In Great Britain the total number of Humps, regardless of absolute height, is almost 3,000!)

An Groban

Approximately two-thirds of the 100 mainland Hughs are Marilyns. This is not surprising, since by their nature Marilyns have greater prominence due to their 150m drop. Of the remainder, around half are Humps. There remain roughly a dozen Hughs which stubbornly refuse to be categorised into the sterile logic of relative height. These include such notable summits as West Kip, Dumgoyne, Ben A'n, Screel Hill, Clachnaben and An Groban. The 150m drop rule is just too restrictive and prescriptive for the Hughs list.

A Note on Classifications

It is perhaps fitting that the acronym HUGHS – Hills Under Graham Height in Scotland – is also the first name of the man whose surname has become a household term for the 3,000ft mountains in Scotland – the Munros.

Sir Hugh Munro could never have imagined how his innocent list of hills would come to dominate the mindset of so many hillwalkers, and lead on to the creation of other lists of hills such as Corbetts, Donalds and Grahams.

During the century since his death, a complete circle has been turned. From Munros (mountains over 3,000ft) to Corbetts (mountains over 2,500ft) to Donalds and Grahams (hills over 2,000ft) – and now, to the Hughs: the best hills under 2,000ft.

As mentioned above, other than the fact that a Hugh is below 2,000 feet, there are no fixed criteria for inclusion. In this sense, Hughs have more in common with Munros, which have no rules for inclusion based on relative height, whereas Corbetts, Grahams and Donalds have strict rules of inclusion based on relative height (re-ascent) and/or other factors.

A Marilyn is any hill in Great Britain (regardless of absolute height) having at least 150m of drop. The list of over 1,500 Marilyns was introduced in Alan Dawson's *The Relative Hills of Britain* (Cicerone, 1992). The Marilyns include the Corbetts and Grahams as subsets, since they require 500ft and 150m of re-ascent respectively. Only slightly over 200 of the 282 Munros are also Marilyns, the rest having re-ascents of less than 150m.

Adding the 200 Hughs to the already existing total of Munros, Corbetts, Grahams and Donalds produces a grand total of 985 listed summits in Scotland. This is a figure which almost begs to be increased to a crisp, round 1,000. Oddly enough, the 100m drop rule applied to mountains over 3,000ft can help out here. As already mentioned, the Munros have no rules for inclusion based on relative height. It turns out that exactly 15 non-Munros over 3,000ft have more than 100m of re-ascent. Many of these have been serious contenders for promotion from 'Top' status to full Munro status and are therefore prominent summits, worthy of inclusion in this 'Scottish Thousand' list.

It is debatable whether this mega-list of 1,000 Scottish hills will ever become a popular objective, except possibly for hardened hill connoisseurs. I hope, however, that the smaller, more manageable list of 200 Hughs will eventually become a popular challenge.

The Right to Roam in Scotland

Responsible right to roam in Scotland has always been at the core of access to wild land and this became law in 2003, when the Land Reform (Scotland) Act enshrined the principle as a statutory right.

For most of the hills described in this book, there are unlikely to be any problems with restricted access, especially south and west of the Great Glen. For some of the more remote hills in the north and west, there may be issues regarding deer stalking, particularly during the main season from 1 July to 20 October. I have never found this a major problem. Details are usually posted at the main access points to the hills, but if in doubt, phone the local Estate office. Note that deer stalking does not take place on Sundays.

Another potential issue is forestry. Some hill routes may be temporarily diverted (but not usually closed) during forestry operations.

Key to Using this Guide

INFORMATION BOXES

Each route description is headed with an Information Box. This concisely itemises the following essential information:

- hill height in metres and in feet
- associated 1:50000 OS map(s)
- 6-figure grid reference of the summit(s)
- total distance (including return height gain)
- estimated completion time(s)
- access point with grid reference
- difficulty
- summary

All of the Hughs are accessible, but the 'Difficulty' and 'Summary' sections in the Information Box provide a quick guide to the characteristics and challenges of individual hills.

SKETCH MAPS

Five location maps show the Hughs by region and each individual route is accompanied by a sketch map designed by the author to be as clear and uncluttered as possible. These maps could in principle be used 'in the field', but when walking it is advisable to have the appropriate OS MAP.

ROUTE QUALITY

The quality of a hill route is, to a large extent, subjective and may be affected by weather conditions, season, etc. The following criteria, satisfied in ratios varying from hill to hill, have been used to select the Hughs:

- prominence
- position
- panorama

Circular routes are generally more satisfying than 'there and back' walks and for each outing every effort has been made to avoid returning exactly the same way, wherever practicable. Possible alternative routes are also sometimes mentioned or described briefly.

NAMES OF HILLS

Where it appears, the derivation of a hill's name is given either in the Information Box or in the narrative describing the route. There is an index of hill names at the end of the book.

PART I

SOUTH AND EAST SCOTLAND – 50 HUGHS

CENTRAL BELT – 26 HUGHS
SOUTHERN UPLANDS – 13 HUGHS
EAST OF THE GREAT GLEN – 11 HUGHS

West Lomond

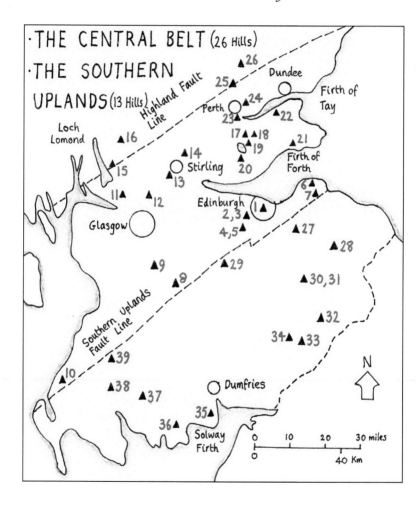

1. ARTHUR'S SEAT (251M/822FT)

MAP	OS SHEET 66 (GR 275729)
DISTANCE	4KM
ASCENT	210M
TIME	1.5–2.5 HRS
ACCESS	PALACE OF HOLYROODHOUSE CAR PARK (GR 271737)
DIFFICULTY	EASY GOING ON EXCELLENT PATHS
SUMMARY	Arthur's Seat is the highest, most prominent and most popular of Edinburgh's seven hills and easily the most climbed hill in Scotland. Its unique position, craggy profile and stunning panoramic views epitomise the very essence of hill 'attitude' – a Capital Hill in every sense.

A half sovereign is smaller than a five shilling piece, and many a Highland Ben of ten times its bulk has less of a real mountain about it than Arthur's Seat.
—Harold Raeburn
(pioneer of Scottish mountaineering)

THE VOLCANIC PLUG of Arthur's Seat is the focus of the extensive Royal Park known as Holyrood Park, and is a striking landmark from all parts of the city and beyond. The name, Arthur's Seat, does not refer to any local of that name, but likely derives from the 12th century, when the powerful legend of King Arthur and his knights caught the imagination of the public, resulting in many places (and hills) being named in his honour.

A road completely surrounds Arthur's Seat within the Park and ascends almost half way up the hill on its eastern side at Dunsapie Loch, where there is ample parking. This is the start of the easiest and quickest ascent, but the described

Arthur's Seat

View from Arthur's Seat

route begins to the north of the hill at the large car park near the Palace of Holyroodhouse and the Scottish Parliament Building. A fee is charged for using this car park.

Leave the car park and cross the road to reach the start of two main walking trails. The one on the right winds its way round the base of an impressive rock formation known as Salisbury Crags and is your return route. Take the left-hand route which ascends gradually and is, oddly enough, not signposted to Arthur's Seat.

After several hundred metres, take a left fork path which heads up through crags to the obvious stone ruin of St Anthony's Chapel, standing on a grassy promenade overlooking St Margaret's Loch. There is an information plaque about the nearby chapel. From here, there is an excellent view of the second most prominent of Edinburgh's seven hills, Calton Hill, with its distinctive Parthenon-type structure.

Leave the Chapel and take a left fork leading downhill at first then rising gradually upwards on the west side of

Whinny Hill, the craggy, flat-shaped eminence on your left. The summit cone of Arthur's seat is visible high above to the right. The path continues upwards into a wide depression curving left at the head over some steeper crags to arrive at a flat grassy platform just below the summit.

Turn right here and follow a path by a chain fence up a series of stone steps. A variety of paths lead to the summit at this point, over polished rock which can be very slippery when wet. Unless you are climbing at night, you are unlikely to have the summit to yourself, but take time to savour the glorious panorama from this rocky perch. Just below the trig point is a view indicator, pointing out scores of surrounding hills such as Bass Rock, North Berwick Law, Traprain Law, the Pentlands and even Ben Lawers in Perthshire. The 'crag and tail' formation of Castle Rock and the Royal Mile is just one of many city landmarks which can be picked out from this phenomenal vantage point.

Immediately south of the summit is the flat, grassy mound known as Nether Hill, which is another good viewpoint. Return to the grassy platform east of the summit and then descend an easy, grassy path on gentle slopes to Dunsapie Loch just beyond the perimeter road. Here you may spot swans and several species of duck.

Turn right and follow the road round the base of Nether Hill, its steep crags on the right clothed in juniper and

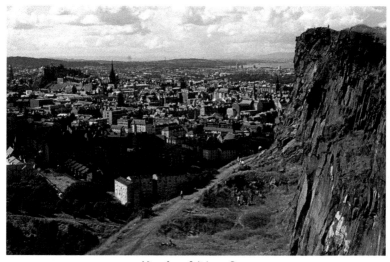

View from Salisbury Crags

gorse. Here, you gain a fine bird's eye view of Duddingston Loch, nestled in greenery in the heart of the city. After about 1km, cross the road and follow another footpath, taking you uphill to the start of Salisbury Crags.

The name 'Salisbury' seems strange for a Scottish location, but the crags may have been named after the Earl of Salisbury who visited here with Edward III in 1335. Others argue that it means 'willows hill' from the Cumbric 'salis bre'.

The path winds round the foot of these crags and is known as the Radical Road, constructed by unemployed weavers in the 19th century. It was here that the geologist James Hutton made the groundbreaking discovery that the crags were formed by the intrusion and cooling of molten rock during volcanic activity.

The final kilometre's stroll round the base of Salisbury Crags is a delight, with ever-changing vistas of Edinburgh's magical skyline backed by the soaring buttresses of basalt to your right. It is also possible to follow a rough path along the top of the crags. For reasons of public safety, climbing on the crags is restricted to a designated area (putting out of bounds some of the best routes in south Scotland).

The Radical Road descends quite steeply in the latter stages down to the road and your starting point.

2. CAERKETTON HILL (478M/1,568FT)
3. ALLERMUIR HILL (493M/1,618FT)

MAP	OS SHEET 66 (GR 237663, 227662)
DISTANCE	5KM
ASCENT	370M
TIME	1.5–2 HRS
ACCESS	SWANSTON (GR 241673)
DIFFICULTY	GRASSY PATHS ON REASONABLE TERRAIN
SUMMARY	Both these hills stand proud at the northern end of the Pentland range and give an unrivalled vista of Edinburgh's sprawling skyline. The traverse of the two is an ideal introduction to the range.

LIKE ARTHUR'S SEAT, the Pentland Hills are held in great affection by Edinburgh folk and have long been a quiet haven of escape from the hustle and bustle of the city far below. The name Pentland is likely derived from the Cumbric (pre-Welsh) *'pen llan'*, meaning height above the enclosed land or church. Caerketton is also of Cumbric origin, *'caer'*

being fort – the eastern shoulder of the hill has remains of a prehistoric fort. Allermuir derives from the Old Scots 'muir', meaning moor.

The old village of Swanston, lying to the south of the A720 Edinburgh bypass, has a peaceful, tranquil air. Robert Louis Stevenson spent many summers here. It makes an ideal base from which to explore the northern end

Allermuir Hill from Caerketton Hill

of the range and there is a walkers' car park at the end of the public road near the golf course.

Follow the path from the left-hand extremity of the car park which soon emerges from trees to the environs of Swanston, a picturesque collection of thatched cottages and colourful gardens. The path continues upwards through a gate and passes to the right of the so-called 'T' Wood.

By now the craggy north face of Caerketton Hill is very prominent. It is the only part of the Pentland Range having a substantial amount of bare rock. At a T-junction, turn left and then fork right soon after on a good path which traverses round to the top of the Hillend Ski Centre. Before this, take a minor path which goes off to the right, climbing steadily to the summit of Caerketton Hill.

Alternatively, continue on round to Hillend and take another ascent path which traverses the eastern shoulder first before ascending to Caerketton Hill. The view of Edinburgh and the Firth of Forth is absolutely stunning on a clear day. Stevenson wrote with great fondness: 'you look over a great expanse of champaign sloping to the sea... So you sit, like Jupiter up on Olympus, and look down from afar on men's life'.

The grassy cone of Allermuir Hill lies 1km to the east and is easily reached from Caerketton by following the twisting ridge by a fence down to a grassy col and a further ascent.

This hill is another fine viewpoint and contains a trig point and a view indicator of dozens of other hills both near and far.

The quickest return route to Swanston is by a path which descends the north-eastern flank of the hill to reach the T-junction just above the 'T' Wood met on the ascent. The time shown above is based on this route.

Alternatively, for a more prolonged outing, descend west by a path to join a well-made vehicle and bicycle track, where you turn right to steeply descend the wooded defile formed by the Howden Burn. Turn right at an old Water Feeder building and follow a grassy track which meanders pleasantly through stands of new trees and passes some established plantations. Note that this is an MOD area and access may be restricted at certain times. Go through a gate and follow a vehicle track past the golf course to reach Swanston Steading. Go left here and right at the road to reach the car park. This alternative route will add around an hour to the total time.

Edinburgh from Caerketton Hill

4. SCALD LAW SCABBED OR PATCHY HILL, SCOTS (579M/1,898FT)
5. WEST KIP SHARP OR POINTED, SCOTS (551M/1,808FT)

MAP	OS SHEET 66 (GR 192611, 178606)
DISTANCE	9KM
ASCENT	410M
TIME	2.5–4 HRS
ACCESS	A702, LAY-BY 1KM FROM SILVERBURN (GR 212608)
DIFFICULTY	GRASSY PATHS ON REASONABLE TERRAIN
SUMMARY	Scald Law, the highest summit of the Pentland Hills, is roughly the central hill of the long, multi-topped ridge stretching from West Kip to Turnhouse Hill in the east. West Kip, together with its neighbour, East Kip, are the most shapely peaks in the Pentlands, both being fine, graceful cones. The circular route described is another fine introduction to these marvellous hills.

IT IS WORTH stating that there is another excellent horseshoe route from the north which takes in both these hills. This starts at the parking area about 2km south of Balerno, near the Threipmuir Reservoir and is slightly longer than the described route. Both routes follow the so-called Kirk Road connecting Penicuik to Balerno.

On the A702 Biggar road, 1km north-east of Silverburn, there is ample parking on two large lay-bys at the foot of the old Kirk Road. This route was used in the past when the parish of Penicuik was extended to Balerno on the north side of the Pentlands where the only kirk was situated. The route is signposted and after a muddy start follows a good grassy path north-west, gradually steepening to reach the col between Scald Law and Carnethy. Ignore the sign saying 'footpath' to the right after 1km. The col is just under 2km from the start.

Climb the fence on the left by a stile and follow the well-established path as it zigzags up the eastern spur of Scald Law. The summit is fairly flat and spacious with a trig point. There are fine views along the ridge back to Carnethy Hill and distant Allermuir Hill, whilst the twin Kips dominate the view to the west.

To continue the round, follow the path west from the summit as it descends to the col below East Kip.

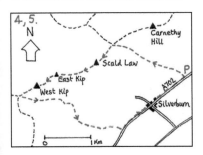

Carnethy Hill from Scald Law

The path, for the latter part of this section, does not follow the ridge line, but instead traverses the northern flank of the hill. In mist, be careful not to stray southwards onto the subsidiary top of South Black Hill with its large cairn. The path ahead is very obvious, going up and over East Kip, then West Kip.

Make the easy ascent of East Kip on a well-used and partly eroded path before a similar, final ascent onto the more rocky summit of West Kip, the last peak of the day. The top of West Kip is in remarkable contrast to that of Scald Law, being very knobbly and pointed, its summit ridge being the narrowest in the Pentlands.

The path descends easily on the west ridge to the wide, grassy col, where you pick up the obvious well-defined path which doubles back below the south flank of West Kip to the farm of Eastside. Beyond here, the path broadens to a wide vehicle track lined by trees which you follow for 1.5km back to the A702.

The only downside is the last 1.5km road-walk to reach the lay-by and the starting point. Note that the northerly horse-shoe route from near Balerno involves no road-walking – try this for a second visit to these great wee hills!

East Kip and West Kip

6. NORTH BERWICK LAW (187M/613FT)

MAP	OS SHEET 66 (GR 556842)
DISTANCE	1.5KM
ASCENT	150M
TIME	0.5–1 HR
ACCESS	THE LAW CAR PARK (GR 553843)
DIFFICULTY	EASY PATH WITH SOME ROCK OUTCROPS
SUMMARY	North Berwick Law has the rare distinction of being the smallest hill in this book. Despite this, the views from the summit of this wee volcanic plug are outstanding and out of all proportion to its modest altitude.

NO VISIT TO the coastal town of North Berwick would be complete without an ascent of 'The Law', as the locals call it. The old Scots word 'law' literally means 'conical hill rising from a surrounding plain'. Rising in craggy magnificence, directly south of the town, it attracts locals and tourists alike and provides a unique opportunity to simply sit and stare from its marvellous summit.

The hill can easily be climbed from the centre of North Berwick and made into a circular tour by the use of a path which runs along the south of the hill, but most people will make use of the purpose-built car park on the west side of the hill. The car park is on the B1347 south of North Berwick and is well signposted.

The first few hundred metres of the walk follow the John Muir Way, a long-distance route across Scotland from Dunbar to Helensburgh. Go through a gate and follow the trail

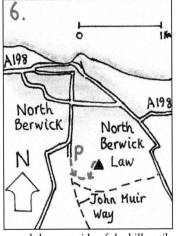

round the west side of the hill until a signposted fork to the left appears. Take this fork as it heads east, before doubling back to gradually wind round the west side of the hill in a rising traverse. Try not to be tempted to take any shortcuts, as erosion on the hill is becoming quite a problem. Higher up, there are numerous rock

North Berwick Law

outcrops, but the path weaves its way upwards to quickly reach the top with its trig point and view indicator perched on a crag.

The most obvious and prominent feature on the hill is the large fibreglass whale jawbone replica which was donated by the 'Friends of North Berwick' in 2008. There had been a real whalebone arch here since 1709, the last one being erected in 1933. By 2005 it was becoming unstable and was removed.

Just below the arch, to the right, is the remains of a Napoleonic Signal Station built in 1803. You will also spot an old concrete World War II observation post directly below the arch. There are also remains of an Iron Age fort, and on the south (landward side) of the hill there is evidence of at least 18 hut circles dating back 2,000 years. Take time to consolidate the wonderful views, both seaward to the islands of Craigleith, Fidra and Bass Rock, and the Fife hills across the Firth of Forth, and landward, across the green fields of East Lothian to the purple haze of the Lammermuirs. Arthur's Seat in Edinburgh is very prominent.

Return by your route of ascent.

View from North Berwick Law

7. TRAPRAIN LAW (221M/725FT)

MAP	OS SHEET 67 (GR 582747)
DISTANCE	1.5KM
ASCENT	120M
TIME	0.5–1 HR
ACCESS	CAR PARK (GR 581749)
DIFFICULTY	EASY ASCENT ON A GRASSY PATH
SUMMARY	This remarkably conspicuous wee hill vies with its northerly cousin, North Berwick Law, as being the most prominent eminence in the area. It is well appreciated from the A1 just a mile north.

TRAPRAIN LAW STANDS in splendid isolation above the rural farmland south of East Linton and west of Dunbar. It has a steep, craggy south-facing escarpment offering a variety of rock-climbing routes. The hill was formed over 300 million years ago and is composed of a laccolith, whereby molten magma was forced upwards causing the surface rocks to swell then solidify. Subsequent glaciation has eroded away many of these surface rocks.

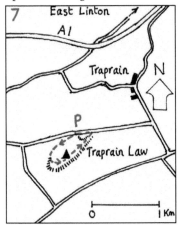

Park on the minor road north of the hill where there is a small lay-by with an information sign and route indicator. This indicator advises you to follow the path which loops round on to the west flank of the hill before ascending to the summit. This takes only 10–15 minutes!

Traprain Law was the site of a late Bronze Age fort having an area of about 10 acres, which was extended around 700 BC when a more substantial stone rampart was constructed, enclosing almost double the original area. In the first century AD the fort was further enlarged to around 40 acres, making it the largest Iron Age fort in south-east Scotland. If you look carefully, the ramparts are still visible in several places.

In Roman times the fort was the chief centre of a tribe known

Traprain Law

as Votadini by the Romans, who, curiously, were allowed to keep the fort and surroundings while other large forts were demolished. In 1919 a large hoard of Roman silver was discovered, dating from 5AD, which is now held in the Museum of Scotland in Edinburgh. There are also several standing stones to the west and south of the hill.

The view north from the trig point is very fine, with the Firth of Forth, the Bass Rock and North Berwick Law all being very prominent on a good day. To the south, the wide blue expanse of the Lammermuir Hills stands proudly above rolling, rural farmland. The Southern Upland Boundary Fault line passes between here and the Lammermuirs, reaching the coast just south of Dunbar.

To make a circuit, continue along the summit ridge heading north-east, passing along the top of a quarry. Take care descending past the quarry on a path with slabby rock, which is slippery when wet. This leads down to the road where you turn left to reach the lay-by.

8. CAIRN TABLE (593M/1,946FT)

MAP	OS SHEET 71 (GR 724242)
DISTANCE	10KM
ASCENT	370M
TIME	2.5–4 HRS
ACCESS	KAMES CAR PARK, SOUTH OF MUIRKIRK (GR 697265)
DIFFICULTY	EASY ANGLED, ILL-DEFINED GRASSY PATHS
SUMMARY	Cairn Table is the highest point of an expansive, wild area south of the village of Muirkirk. Like Tinto Hill further east, it has a substantial cairn on its domed summit and is a prominent landmark for miles around. Not surprisingly, the summit views are extensive and wide-ranging.

THE ONLY PRACTICABLE approach to this hill is from Muirkirk to the north-west of Cairn Table on the A70 Lanark to Cumnock road. From Cumnock, drive down Furnace Road to Kames where there is a walkers' car park on the left. An information board shows this to be a popular walking area with long-distance routes to Sanquhar and Wanlockhead. The described route is indicated in red.

Take the path at the end of the car park and fork left before crossing a stile. Stay on the grassy path as it weaves its way round grassy hummocks and old mine workings, crossing several boggy parts on duckboards. The pointed cairn on the summit of Cairn Table is obvious in clear weather.

The warbling skylark high above is a common sight, as is the curlew with its plaintive cry. The area is also one of the most significant strongholds of Hen Harriers in Europe but in recent years numbers have decreased and CCTV cameras are being used to catch egg-snatchers.

The path steepens and crosses more stony ground before reaching the summit, 4km from the car park. The summit trig point is also accompanied by a view indicator and two substantial cairns, the most westerly

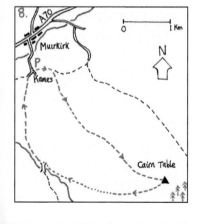

The summit of Cairn Table

being a Great War memorial cairn. On a clear day the views are excellent with the cone of Tintoretto Hill very prominent to the east. West and south, Ailsa Craig, Arran and the Galloway Hills are all potentially visible.

For those with time, inclination and spare energy, it makes a good round trip to continue south via Grindstone Rig to Stony Hill and then west to Wardlaw Hill where there is another memorial cairn to a war casualty.

The described route, however, follows a path starting from the back of the memorial cairn leading south-west then veering west past several cairns, descending gradually through heather and grass on the vague western spur of

the hill. The path soon turns north-west lower down to a bridge over the Garpel Water. From here, follow a rough vehicle track on the east side of the river.

Near the end of this track you will pass a cairn built in memory of John Loudon Macadam, the inventor of tarmacadam. The area is the site of several tar kilns and it is possible to partake in an audiovisual tour of the old workings. Further on, the large ruined house on the left was his residence and the first-ever tarmac road constructed forms the last part of the walk, which leads directly to the car park.

9. LOUDOUN HILL (316M/1,037FT)

MAP	OS SHEET 71 (GR 609379)
DISTANCE	1KM
ASCENT	120M
TIME	0.5–1 HR
ACCESS	SPIRIT OF SCOTLAND SCULPTURE CAR PARK (GR 613379)
DIFFICULTY	SHORT AND EASY ASCENT ON AN INTERMITTENT PATH
SUMMARY	The dramatic rocky profile of Loudoun Hill standing just north of the A71 between Strathaven and Darvel draws the eye and imparts a might and majesty out of all proportion to its lowly height.

THE ANCIENT REMNANT of a volcanic plug, Loudoun Hill is like a smaller version of Arthur's Seat in Edinburgh. It is also the site of some stirring episodes in Scottish history and a memorial sculpture at its base is a reflection of these turbulent times.

Drive down the minor road north of the A71 signposted 'Loudon Hill and Spirit of Scotland Sculpture'. There is a car park on the left after 1km. An information sign gives details

of two battles fought here during the Wars of Independence (Wallace in 1297 and Robert the Bruce in 1307).

Follow the path going along to the modern sculpture which you will either like or loathe! There is a grand view of the craggy eastern ramparts of the hill rearing up above the gentle grassy lower slopes dotted with gorse bushes.

Continue on the path as it drops down to cross River Irvine by a wooden bridge. Follow a grassy track which contours round the base of the hill to the left (south). At a ruined house on the left a small path branches off to the right and this should be followed upwards by a fence and over a dry stone wall to a wooded area. A faint, grassy path then forks off to the right to reach the summit with a trig point.

Enjoy far-reaching views of the surrounding countryside and try to ignore the serried ranks of wind turbines to the north at Whitelees.

Loudoun Hill

To return by a different route, descend north into a wooded copse to pick up a faint path which takes you back round to the gentle lower slopes of the hill and the wooden bridge used on the ascent. Return to the car park via the memorial sculpture.

The summit of Loudoun Hill

10. KNOCKDOLIAN (265M/871FT)

MAP	OS SHEET 76 (GR 113848)
DISTANCE	2KM
ASCENT	210M
TIME	1 HR
ACCESS	B7044 LAY-BY (GR 120848)
DIFFICULTY	FIELD AND EASY GRASSY PATH
SUMMARY	The craggy and shapely cone of Knockdolian is a prominent south Ayrshire landmark with unrivalled coastal views to Ailsa Craig and Arran. This is a fine hill to climb on a late summer's evening when the sun is sinking in the west.

KNOCKDOLIAN HAS OFTEN been compared to its island cousin of Ailsa Craig and indeed, is sometimes referred to as the 'False Craig'. Both are volcanic plugs and useful landmarks for sailors entering or leaving the Firth of Clyde. 'Knock', from the Gaelic '*cnoc*', refers to the hill's knoll-like shape and relative isolation. The origin of 'dolian' is obscure.

The hill stands halfway between

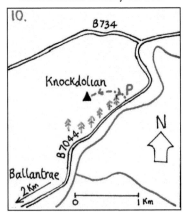

the sleepy villages of Ballantrae and Colmonell and north of the river Stinchar. It is only just in the Central Lowlands region of Scotland, the boundary fault separating this from the Southern Uplands, running from Ballantrae to Dunbar on the east coast.

Park at a lay-by opposite a cottage on the B7044 Ballantrae to Colmonell road. This lay-by is due east of the summit and there is a sign indicating the route to the top about 100m eastwards along the road.

Walk up the road to the sign and go through a gate into a large green, sloping field where you should spot another exit gate up to the left. If there is livestock in the field then keep to the fence on the left until you reach the top gate. You may wish to visit the site of an old Iron Age fort marked on the map a few hundred metres further round the hill.

Go through the gate and follow a grassy path through bracken, taking a

Knockdolian

rough line up the north-east ridge of the hill. At times, the path branches off into various sheep-tracks, but the route is fairly obvious and soon reaches the grassy summit with a trig point and small cairn.

The top is a marvellous viewpoint for the Ayrshire coast and seawards to the iconic stump of Ailsa Craig backed by Kintyre and Arran. Eastwards, the rolling, rural Ayrshire farmland and pockets of trees form a wonderful green patchwork.

It is best to return by the route of ascent.

Ailsa Craig from Knockdolian

II. DUMGOYNE (427M/1,400FT)

MAP	OS SHEET 64 (GR 542828)
DISTANCE	7KM
ASCENT	470M
TIME	2.5–3.5 HRS
ACCESS	DISTILLERY LAY-BY OR CAR PARK (GR 527826)
DIFFICULTY	REASONABLE GRASSY PATH, STEEPENING NEAR SUMMIT
SUMMARY	The volcanic plug of Dumgoyne (Fort of Arrows) is a dramatic bookend at the western end of the Campsies and a prominent landmark for miles around. It is the most distinctive hill of the range and also the most popular.

LYING DIRECTLY NORTH of Glasgow, the Campsie Fells (Crooked Seat Hills) form a high, rolling, grassy plateau and are generally fairly featureless, with only a few distinctive tops. For Glasgow folk, however, they have always represented a wild, yet welcoming, northern frontier and a place to escape from the daily urban grind into an oasis of fresh air and freedom. Along with Arthur's Seat

in Edinburgh, Dumgoyne is likely to be many would-be hillwalkers' first experience of the great outdoors.

Dumgoyne is generally ascended from two main starting points, the Glengoyne Distillery on the A81 to the west of the hill, or Blanefield to the south. The route from the distillery is shorter and in the walk described here, includes the little brother of Dumgoyne, the less visited Dumfoyne, as part of a fine circular route.

Either park in the lay-by opposite the distillery or use the distillery car park. To the right of the distillery is a wide grassy slope which is accessed by a gap in the fence. Walk through the gap and upwards, to cross a stile and follow a grass path up to a vehicle track crossing from left to right. This track is known as the 'Pipe Road' and is the line of the water supply from Loch Katrine, in the Trossachs, to Glasgow.

Continue uphill on the same grass

Dumgoyne

path and reach open hillside by crossing two stiles with a small burn between them. Take the left of two obvious muddy paths which ascend the steep hillside. Higher up, this path turns right to make a steady, rising traverse of the western flank, eventually levelling off slightly on a shoulder with several false summits. Continue upwards on easier ground, before a final steepening to the summit.

The fairly small, flat summit area contains a large boulder which was helicoptered in with financial help from the Rotary Club of Strathendrick. A view indicator on top of the boulder has sadly disappeared and begs the question – why would anybody want to pilfer it?

The top commands glorious views northwards to island-studded Loch Lomond, with the elegant profile of Ben Lomond dominating the skyline. The hazy urban sprawl of Glasgow to the south is in stark contrast. The view east is blocked by the higher, grassy slopes of the Campsie Fells and for those who want a longer walk, the highest point of Earl's Seat can be reached, but is little more than a slight swelling of the moor with limited views.

More enticing is the little hill of Dumfoyne (possibly 'hill fort of the wart') to the south-east which is the next objective and gives a great view of Dumgoyne. Descend by a fairly steep path (which zigzags down the north-east slope) and pick up the path heading north-east which would

The summit of Dumgoyne

take you to Earl's Seat. In about 500m, strike off to the right along a grassy ridge on a vague all-terrain-vehicle track. This heads directly to the summit of Dumfoyne, where the craggy eastern face of Dumgoyne is well seen.

Descend south from here on fairly steep, grassy slopes to pick up a path which contours along the base of the two hills. Turn left, and follow the path over a stile and two streams before it starts to descend by a fine wooded gorge and through a gate. A gate lower down leads to the Pipe Road and a bridge near Cantywheery Cottage, where you turn right.

The Pipe Road swings round to the right past a cottage before entering a wood. Just over 1km of pleasant woodland walking takes you to a gate and the open field leading back to the distillery by the outward grassy path.

12. MEIKLE BIN (570M/1,870FT)

MAP	OS SHEET 57 OR 64 (GR 667822)
DISTANCE	13KM
ASCENT	350M
TIME	3–4 HRS
ACCESS	LAY-BY AT NORTH END OF CARRON VALLEY RESERVOIR (OS SHEET 57; GR 673859)
DIFFICULTY	MAINLY FOREST TRACKS AND GENTLE GRASSY SLOPES
SUMMARY	Meikle Bin translates as 'muckle ben' or 'big hill' and second to Dumgoyne is the most 'pointy' hill in the Campsies, with wonderful views across Glasgow, the Clyde Estuary to Ailsa Craig and Arran.

THOUGH THE UPPER cone of Meikle Bin is free of trees, the hill is surrounded by commercial forestry on all sides, but this should not put you off the ascent of what is a very fine hill. There are three main points of access to the hill: from the south over the Kilsyth Hills from near Queenzieburn; from the west on the Crow Road at Waterhead; or from the north starting at the northern end of the Carron Valley Reservoir. The latter (the described route) has little or no route-finding problems: despite the forestry, this circular route gives fairly open views of the surrounding countryside. Note that the whole circular route will require both OS maps 57 and 64 but returning by the same way would only require map 57.

Park on the B818 Denny to Fintry road at a large lay-by opposite the entrance to Todholes Farm at the north-western extremity of Carron

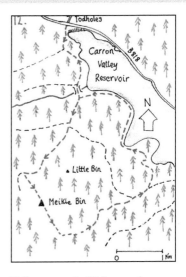

Valley reservoir. Walk past the green barrier and follow the vehicle track through mixed woodland, past the dam and onwards through the forest, ignoring any right-hand turn-offs. After about 1.5km cross the river Carron

Meikle Bin

by a bridge and take a right-hand turn about 200m later. Follow this track as it gradually ascends, ignoring a right and a left turn. The path steepens slightly, climbing the northern flank of Little Bin, a subsidiary summit of Meikle Bin. The track eventually begins to bend left then right, continuing round the northern spur of Meikle Bin. You will soon pass a muddy firebreak on the left with a small cairn. This marks the start of one path onto the summit ridge, but by continuing on you should arrive at a signpost where a better grassy path soon leads out of the trees and onto the easy-angled north-west ridge of Meikle Bin. An easy grassy ridge-walk leads in 700m to the trig point, where you can relax and enjoy the magnificent summit panorama.

To continue the circular walk, follow the line of the ridge in a south-easterly direction to the forest edge. Descend a rather muddy firebreak, crossing two drainage ditches by old railway sleepers before turning left into a second firebreak. This leads in

about 0.5km to the start of a forestry track. There may well be several fallen trees in this second firebreak so prepare for some ducking and diving!

Follow this track downhill through more open forest, passing a junction after about 1.5km. Some 300m later, take a left-hand fork which crosses a stream by a bridge. This narrower track meanders its way along the south shore of the reservoir where, if you are lucky, you may spot some wildfowl. In about 3km, you will arrive back at the bridge over River Carron where you follow the outward track back to the start.

1.   The summit of Meikle Bin

13. LEWIS HILL (266M/873FT)

MAP	OS SHEET 57 (GR 761888)
DISTANCE	10KM
ASCENT	250M
TIME	2.5–3.5 HRS
ACCESS	NORTH THIRD NORTHERLY PARKING AREA (GR 771907) OTHER CLOSER ACCESS POINTS ARE POSSIBLE
DIFFICULTY	NARROW PATHS WITH SEVERAL STEEP SECTIONS
SUMMARY	This fine, craggy and wooded hill is the high point of a long rocky escarpment lying to the east of North Third Reservoir to the south-west of Stirling. A traverse of the escarpment and a circuit of the reservoir make an excellent circular route with wonderful views.

LEWIS HILL (ORIGIN UNCERTAIN) is commonly regarded as being part of the Touch Hills (pronounced 'Tooch' Hills with a guttural 'ch') which are themselves part of the Campsies range. The name 'Touch' is a corruption of the Gaelic '*tulach*' meaning a knoll or hill.

The hill and reservoir form the focus of a number of scenic circular walks which are very popular with Stirling folk, the city being only a few kilometres away. I was first introduced to this hill by an old friend and Stirling resident by the name of Andy Oldfield; on that dreich hogmanay, it still exuded great charm.

The described route begins at the parking area given above, which is easily reached from Stirling or from Cambusbarron, west of the M9. There is a signpost for North Third Reservoir and you should follow

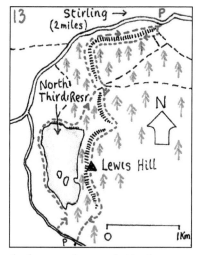

the forest track over a bridge for about 100m before taking a left fork. Almost immediately, turn right, where a narrow path goes uphill between two large boulders. Turn right again almost immediately to climb uphill on

Lewis Hill

a narrow slabby path leading upwards through birch trees to the start of the escarpment walk.

Follow the edge of the escarpment with a steep drop to your right as it continues westward. You will catch glimpses of a more substantial track down to your left, running parallel with this one. This is the track you left before climbing uphill.

The path begins to swing southward after about 1km and there are several sections of steep ascent and descent, before it drops down to cross a forest track at a break in the cliffs. The path continues on the other side and is indicated by a post with an arrow.

The next section of clifftop walking is the most sensational of the entire

route. There are some unusual rock formations with grand views looking out to the Munros of Ben Vorlich and Stuc a'Chroin, together with the shapely form of Ben Ledi.

Descend to a second break in the cliffs before crossing a minor track and taking a left fork leading back up onto the ridge crest. The arrowed route right goes to North Third Reservoir. Pass the remains of an old fort and continue for another 0.5km to the summit of Lewis Hill, where there is a trig point. Enjoy marvellous views across North Third Reservoir with its two wooded islands.

The path continues southward, gradually descending through an area of newly felled trees, before eventually reaching the minor road and small car park south of the reservoir. Turn right here and go along the road for a few hundred metres before turning off right on a path just before a bridge over a stream. This leads toward the south end of the reservoir and crosses the stream by a concrete bridge.

Continue pleasantly along the western shore of the reservoir crossing several wooden bridges and duck-boards. At the north end follow the path along the dam and turn left along a path to gain a forestry track heading north. At an obvious cairn, turn left along a minor path which winds its way through trees directly beneath the crags of the northern escarpment. There are numerous ruins of old limekiln workings dotted about near this path.

View from Lewis Hill ridge

After about 1.5km you will arrive back at your starting point to complete a satisfying circuit.

14. DUMYAT (418M/1,371FT)

MAP	OS SHEET 57, 58
DISTANCE	5KM
ASCENT	400M
TIME	1.5–2.5 HRS (DESCRIBED ROUTE)
ACCESS	DESCRIBED ROUTE: BLAIRLOGIE CAR PARK (GR 831968)
	EASIEST ROUTE: SHERIFFMUIR ROAD LAY-BY (GR813980)
	OR MENSTRIE (GR 848970)
DIFFICULTY	STEEP ASCENT BY DESCRIBED ROUTE – EASIER OPTIONS AVAILABLE
SUMMARY	The volcanic plug of Dumyat is to the Ochils, what Dumgoyne is to the Campsies. Its rocky and distinctive profile has given it the honour of the most popular peak in the range, despite its relatively modest height.

AS THE CAMPSIES are Glasgow's hills and the Pentlands are Edinburgh's hills, the Ochils are Stirling's hills. They extend for about 30km from Stirling almost to Perth and form an effective barrier between these two cities. The name Ochil derives from the old Celtic word '*uchel*' meaning high ground and indeed the main summits are around 500 feet higher than that of the Campsies or Pentlands, with several Donalds (over 2,000ft).

Dumyat stands aloof and separate from its higher, grassier neighbours and its position at the western edge of the range give it its unrivalled views overlooking Stirling and the Forth Valley. Pronounced 'dum-eye-att', the name is probably from the fort or dun of the Maente tribe and there is in fact Pictish remains of a fort on the south-wesr top of the hill.

Despite its distinctive profile and lowly stature, Dumyat is topographically quite a complex wee hill with a variety of different routes to its summit, some quick and easy, others more demanding. Its richness will amply reward several separate visits. The described circular route samples much of the character of the hill, though involves

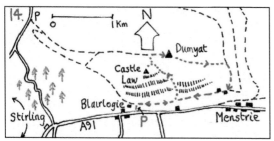

Dumyat from Stirling

a fair amount of steep walking. For those who would prefer a quick 'there and back' with only half the amount of ascent the Sheriffmuir road lay-by approach from the west is the option to take.

Between the hillfoot villages of Blairlogie and Menstrie, the south face of Dumyat rises up steeply in craggy tiers split by an obvious grassy gully known as Warlock Glen. This glen separates the main summit of the hill from the south-west top known as Castle Law. The described route ascends this gully to the top before descending the easy, grassy, east slopes of the hill and returning by a pleasant track running below the crags.

Blairlogie car park is situated just north of the A91 Hillfoots road, less than a mile from the roundabout to the west. From the car park, head north upwards and over a stile to a track which runs from east to west along the base of the hill. Turn right along the track and take a left fork after 50m. Follow this path for several hundred metres until you are past a large mass of gorse bushes on the left.

Turn off left at this point up a faint grassy path heading for an obvious large crag. Gradually move to the left of the crag and climb easy slopes to reach a more well-defined path above the crag. This path climbs up into the now quite pronounced jaws of Warlock Glen, really more of a cavernous gorge with dramatic crags on either side. Stay in the gorge, ignoring any side trails which soon lead to precarious situations! The path crosses a burn several times

Dumyat

before soon reaching boggy ground at the top of the gully.

At this point it is worth making a small detour left to walk the short distance to Castle Law, the site of an ancient Pictish fort where there are fine views and more chance of having the top to yourself than at the true summit, which is visible from here.

Heading north from Castle Law will bring you onto the westerly Sheriffmuir road approach path in less than 0.5km. Turn right on the path and reach the main summit of Dumyat with its trig point perched on a craggy outcrop. The summit also has a large millennium beacon fire basket and a plaque to the Argyll and Sutherland Highlanders.

After a well-deserved rest and enjoyment of the view, head north-east of the summit for about 10m to pick up a path which zigzags downwards on easy, grassy slopes in a direction just south of east. This is quite a popular route (from Menstrie) and in clear weather should be fairly obvious. Within 1km this path reaches a vehicle track where you should turn right and gradually loop round to the right past Dumyat Farm where the imposing craggy south face of Dumyat becomes very obvious. When you reach the burn at the foot of the Warlock Glen you will need to branch off to the right at the Dumyat Farm sign, crossing the burn by the small footbridge. The path leads back to the original track and the stile to the car park.

15. CONIC HILL (361M/1,184FT)

MAP	OS SHEET 56 (GR 433924)
DISTANCE	5KM
ASCENT	330M
TIME	1.5–2.5 HRS
ACCESS	BALMAHA CAR PARK
DIFFICULTY	GOOD PATH WITH STEPPED SECTIONS
SUMMARY	Conic Hill is one of the most popular wee hills in Scotland, and for good reason. Its summit is on the Highland Boundary Fault line, only a stone's throw from the iconic West Highland Way. Its commanding position above Loch Lomond makes for summit views out of all proportion to its modest height.

THE NAME CONIC HILL does not refer to its vaguely conical shape when viewed from Balmaha, but derives from the Gaelic '*coinneach*' meaning 'mossy' or 'boggy'. On the approach to Balmaha from Drymen, the hill appears as a long, knobbly ridge with several distinct tops and gives the impression of a much higher hill than its height would suggest.

Sadly, many folk climb Conic Hill as a 'plan B' when perhaps rain and cloud obscure the top of the bigger prize of Munro Ben Lomond further up the road. Climbing Conic Hill on a poor day does not do the hill justice, however, and it should really be saved for a sunny day.

Begin at the large car park in Balmaha where there is a visitor centre. At the back of the car park at an information sign go up some steps to reach a track, where you turn right – you are now on the West Highland

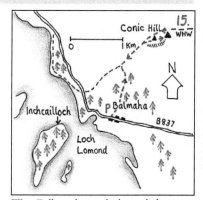

Way. Follow the track through forest for about 400m before turning left at a junction (there is a WHW marker post here).

The trail begins to climb here, eventually reaching a set of wooden steps and a gate at the forest edge. Go through the gate and stay on the path as it winds round to the left and upwards on several more stepped sections. The obvious knoll on the

Conic Hill

left is the first of Conic Hill's many tops and forms part of the Highland Boundary Fault line.

Reach a flat section at a col where you should spot the path's continuation on a series of stone steps ascending to the right in a slight depression. Climb the stone steps to reach a small flat area where there are marvellous views north and west out across the expanse of Loch Lomond.

From here, the path (still on the WHW) makes a rising traverse of the north-western flank of the hill on a natural shelf which bypasses the main ridge-line. As you climb higher, the view in reverse gives an excellent appreciation of the line of the Boundary Fault, which is marked by the obvious linearity in the islands of Inchcailloch, Torrinch, Creinch and Inchmurrin – these all lie on the Fault Line. In the far distance beyond the

loch is the peak of Ben Bowie above Helensburgh, also on the Fault. On a clear day, you may even spot the isle of Arran, it too being part of the Fault.

There are one or two indistinct paths forking off to the right which lead on to the ridge-line and these may be used, but the main one appears at a level section about 0.5km from the top of the stone steps. This climbs directly up over some knobbly outcrops of conglomerate rocks to a flat, grassy area before a short, steep pull to the flat top, marked as 358m on the OS map. This is often classed as the summit, but in fact the highest point (at 361m) is the second knoll north-east of here, easily reached in 10 minutes by a path following the ridge-line. A small cairn marks the summit.

The view is dominated by Loch Lomond and the arc of Munros

Loch Lomond from Conic Hill

beyond, with Ben Lomond rising like a sentinel, stealing the show. Southwards, the line of the Campsies is very obvious with the volcanic plug of Dumgoyne the prominent feature. The distinction between Lowland and Highland landscapes is perhaps nowhere better appreciated than from the summit of Conic Hill.

Descend by dropping north to pick up the WHW in five minutes and return by your route of ascent. It is possible to vary the route by picking up another path at the top of the stone steps which descend a minor spur known as Druim nan Buraich, reaching the road about 1km north of Balmaha. However, this path is less distinct and is boggy in the lower reaches.

The fine viewpoint known as Craigie Fort is also worth visiting and only adds another half hour. On arriving back at the car park, stay on the WHW for about five minutes until it reaches the road. Cross the road and follow the path right onto a minor road passing two cottages. Just beyond, follow a path going up the wooded hill on the right (marked by WHW signpost). This leads to a marvellous rocky viewpoint of the loch; there is also a good view of Conic Hill.

Continue on the path as it descends to the lochside where you turn left and cross a metal bridge, enjoying the fine views across the loch. This leads to a small pier and the end of the minor road with the two cottages. Follow the road and path back to Balmaha.

16. BEN A'N OR A'AN ORIGINALLY AM BINNEIN, PINNACLE OR POINT OR BEANNAN, LITTLE MOUNTAIN (454M/1,489FT)

MAP	OS SHEET 57 (GR 502082)
DISTANCE	3KM
ASCENT	350M
TIME	2–3 HRS
ACCESS	BEN A'N CAR PARK (GR 509070) ON THE A821 NORTH OF LOCH ACHRAY
DIFFICULTY	EXCELLENT PATH WITH A STEEP STEPPED SECTION
SUMMARY	Quite simply, one of the finest 'wee hills' in Scotland. Its rocky mountainous profile rising from the woods and lochs of the Trossachs, together with the sublime summit panorama give it the air of a much higher peak.

AS AN INTRODUCTION to the Scottish hills Ben A'n cannot be bettered.

Ben A'n is the jewel in the crown of the Trossachs, the land of forests, lochs and hills so beloved of Sir Walter Scott and immortalised in his poem 'The Lady of the Lake', referring to Loch Katrine, which lies to the west of Ben A'n. The Gaelic derivation of Trossachs is *'na troiseachan'*, meaning 'crossing place', and was originally the small neck of land between Loch Katrine and

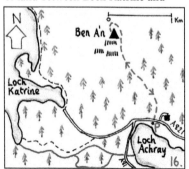

Loch Achray where boats had to be porteraged. The Trossachs now refers to the expansive area of scenic beauty between Callander and Aberfoyle.

Ben A'n is best appreciated from the north side of the Duke's Pass on the A821 north of Aberfoyle where its grand, rocky southern ramparts rise high above the placid waters of Loch Achray. The hill itself is actually just a minor top of the higher and rather nondescript summit of Meall Gainmheich, a Marilyn. It says much that I have ascended Ben A'n on dozens of occasions but have only been up Meall Gainmheich once.

The route of ascent follows an easy but steep footpath all the way to the summit. Cross the road from the car park and follow the path upwards through a forest of spruce, larch, birch and Scots Pine, going over a burn by a wooden bridge higher up. After about half an hour, emerge

Ben A'n

all grades.

Luckily, the path avoids the crags and takes a sneaky route up the east (right) side of the hill by a stream via a section of stepping-stones. Higher up, the stream is crossed and the path becomes more rocky with boulders before going round the back of the hill on more level heathery terrain.

A final short but steep little pull takes you up to the small summit ridge. The actual summit is formed by a sharp blade of rock on the west side, below which is the popular 10-second slab, a smooth,

from the trees to a flat, grassy area where you gain your first proper view of the imposing south face of Ben A'n.

I once took school-kids up here and one declared loudly, 'We can't go up there – that's rock climbing!' She was not that far off the mark as these are indeed numerous recorded climbs of

but not entirely hold-less rock slab which good climbers can scale in ten seconds. Try it at your own risk!

The view from here is truly memorable, particularly of Loch Katrine to the west, backed by higher, possibly snow-covered Munros. The Graham of Ben Venue is very obvious

Loch Katrine from Ben A'n

across Loch Katrine to the south-west.

Competent hillwalkers may want to descend by a different route and this is possible by a rather vague and sometimes slippery path heading north then west from the summit leading down to Loch Katrine. It is advisable, however, to descend by the route of ascent.

17. WEST LOMOND (522M/1,713FT)

MAP	OS SHEET 58 (GR 197066)
DISTANCE	8KM
ASCENT	360M
TIME	2–4 HRS
ACCESS	DESCRIBED ROUTE: GLEN VALE CAR PARK (GR 173069)
	DIRECT ROUTE: CRAIGMEAD CAR PARK (GR 227062)
DIFFICULTY	SOME SECTIONS OF VAGUE, GRASSY PATHS
SUMMARY	West Lomond is the highest and most prominent peak of the Lomond Hills (Beacon Hills), a concise group of four distinct hills presenting steep and inviting northern and western profiles rising abruptly from the farm lands of Fife. The view from the summit is stunning, so climb this on a clear day!

THE CONICAL SUMMIT dome of West Lomond is a well-known landmark for miles around and the twin summits of East and West Lomond are often easily identifiable from many Highland hills.

The popular route up West Lomond begins east of the hill at Craigmead car park on the hill road between Falkland and Leslie. The car park is at a height of 300m so only a little over 200m of ascent is required to reach the summit. However, the approach involves a 3km trudge across fairly featureless moorland, albeit on a good path, and returns the same way. The route does not really do the hill justice and misses out on some remarkable geological oddities.

The described route is a satisfying and interesting circular walk from the west, where the full character of the hill can be appreciated. The

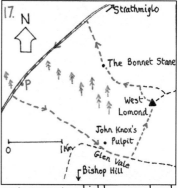

route passes two highly unusual rock formations with interesting geological and historical backgrounds.

Begin at the small car park on the minor road connecting Glenlomond and Strathmiglo – this is an official cycling route. The car park is 2km from Glenlomond just beyond a small wood on the right. On leaving the car park you will need to walk along the road (left) for about 300m to reach the start of the Glen Vale path which is marked by a signpost. The well-trodden path passes through the wood initially, before meandering its way upwards by Glen Burn, where the steep and (in places) craggy slopes of West Lomond's north-western flank are very prominent.

Higher up, go through a gate and enter the steep-sided Glen Vale, hemmed in by the slopes of West Lomond on the left and Bishop Hill on the right. Ahead is the first of two geological curiosities known as John Knox's Pulpit, an impressive gnarled sandstone outcrop which stands about 30m above the path and contains a shallow cave formed by a ledge and overhang. It is easy to access the cave by a short, steep path starting just beyond the crag.

It is said that the ledge was used by Knox as a speaking platform whilst addressing the persecuted supporters of the Reformation and the glen is also known as the Covenanter's Glen. Nowadays the ledge makes an excellent lunch stop!

Continue upwards through the narrowing cleft of the glen and onto flatter, more boggy terrain until you reach a rough vehicle track near a gate on the opposite side of the burn. Turn left onto the track for about 50m before branching off to the left on a grassy path which heads directly up the south flank of West Lomond. Off to the left, and higher up from here is a rocky escarpment known as the Devil's Burdens. You may wish to make a detour to visit it. The path goes initially over tussocky, boggy ground before the final steep, grassy climb to the summit crowned by a large cairn and a trig point.

The mosaic patchwork of Fife farmland and the distant Highlands draw the eye whilst the cone of East Lomond is prominent to the east. After soaking up the incredible view take the path from the summit heading west, which gradually curves round to

West Lomond

The Bonnet Stane

descend steeply in a northerly direction. This path begins to contour round the hill until East Lomond becomes visible and you will meet another path. Head east on this path for about 200m until a less well-defined path branches off to the left to descend into a step cleft. This can be quite tricky to find, but as you descend, an obvious circular pond should be visible far below which is a good guide. This is unmarked on the OS map.

Below the cleft, the path contours along the hillside, crossing a fence and then following a second fence before dropping down to a large green field where the second of the walk's geological features is situated. This is the so-called Bonnet Stane, a curious lump of calciferous sandstone where differential weathering has sculpted a mushroom-shaped rock with a three-ton slab (the bonnet) perched precariously on top of an impossibly narrow pillar. Below the Bonnet is the Maiden's Bower, a little cave-like room carved out of the sandstone which reputedly was home to a local lass whose lover was murdered. You can read about this and other legends on a plaque at the entrance to the cave.

From the Bonnet Stane, head north-west to an obvious gap in the dyke with a post. From here, turn right and follow a rough vehicle track which gradually becomes more well-defined as it runs to the left of a fence and dyke. Cross a fence by a stile and continue to stay on the track until it reaches the road in less than 1km. Turn left at the road and follow it for less than 2km to reach your starting point.

18. EAST LOMOND (448M/1471FT)

MAP	OS SHEET 59; 58 ALSO REQUIRED (GR 244062)
DISTANCE	7KM
ASCENT	380M
TIME	2–4 HRS
ACCESS	DESCRIBED ROUTE: FALKLAND VILLAGE CAR PARK (GR 254073)
	POPULAR ROUTE: CRAIGMEAD CAR PARK (GR 227062)
	QUICKEST ROUTE: PURIN HILL CAR PARK (GR 252059)
	LONGEST ROUTE: PITCAIRN CAR PARK, GLENROTHES (GR 267035)
DIFFICULTY	STEEP ASCENT BY DESCRIBED ROUTE – EASIER OPTIONS AVAILABLE
SUMMARY	Like its neighbour West Lomond 5km to the west, East Lomond, also known as Falkland Hill, is an ancient volcanic stump. It stands guard over the historic and picturesque village of Falkland. The view from the summit is wonderful, arguably better than that from West Lomond, East Lomond being closer to the Firth of Forth.

THE ASCENT OF East Lomond can be made from four separate starting points as given above. Each has its merits and drawbacks, but the circular route described gives a full appreciation of this fine little hill, ascending from Falkland village and descending by the popular route. If you intend to climb both East and West Lomond together, then the Craigmead car park, lying between the two summits at a height of 300m, provides the best starting point.

The ascent from Falkland village is unrelentingly steep, though on a reasonable path. Some may prefer the described route in reverse, with a long gradual ascent first, followed by a steep descent. The choice is yours. Finally, if you're feeling really lazy and want to see the view with the minimum of effort then park at the Purin Hill car park to the east, where you only have 1km of walking and an ascent of 100m to reach the top – a bit of a cheat really.

The walk begins in Falkland car park, which is signposted, and is

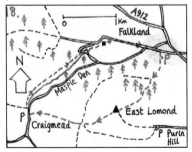

East Lomond from Falkland Village

situated west of High Street along a narrow road known as Back Wynd. The car park is on the left further up and holds nearly 100 vehicles.

Leave the car park and turn left along Back Wynd up to an old factory building which manufactured linen when weaving was a big industry in the area. It now makes plastic bags – changing times. Turn right at the factory, then left up a hill (East Loan) to join a gravel footpath signposted East Lomond.

Bear right at a fork then branch off left up a flight of wooden steps into beech and pine woodland – all signposted to Lomond Hills. Ignore a path branching to the right and continue upwards as the path swings to the right before ascending a long flight of steps with a handrail to the edge of the wood.

The summit is now in view and the path bears right to climb up steeply to a stile. The final 100m to the top is the steepest part of the walk and you will no doubt be relieved to reach the flat summit with its view indicator.

The actual height of East Lomond is a case of confusion, owing to the fact that the trig point is curiously situated on the southern shoulder of the hill, 24m below the actual summit, which is 448m high – not 434m, as shown on some maps.

The view indicator picks out scores of obvious landmarks and others not so obvious, and on a clear day you should be able to spot Largo Law to the east, the Bass Rock and North

Falkland fron East Lomond

Berwick Law to the south-east, and the line of the Grampians far to the north. The view west is dominated by West Lomond.

To continue the walk, descend a grassy path to the south shoulder to visit the trig point, before following a wide path south-west which descends fairly steeply to a long, level section by a fence. Go through a gate and follow the track between two dry stone walls.

An interesting diversion can be made just after the gate, round a guided walk visiting old limekilns, where excavated lime was fired to provide enrichment for the surrounding fields.

Continue along the track with the huge bulk of West Lomond directly ahead. The large monument standing above trees to the north-west is a memorial to Tyndall Bruce, once keeper of the Falkland Palace and builder of the gothic church in the village in 1850, where there is a bronze statue of him.

Reach the Craigmead car park and hill road, where you turn right. About 200m down the road, turn left along a path with a West Lomond sign. Almost immediately, turn right along a well-constructed gravel track, passing through an area of felled forest. This is part of a fairly recently constructed network of paths around Upper Maspie Den, which link with paths in Falkland Estate lower down.

At a fork in the path either can be taken, but the left fork gives fine

views looking across to East Lomond
from the west side of the Maspie
Burn. Lower down, reach a muddy
vehicle track where you turn right.
Just before the bridge, take a left
fork, keeping the burn on your right.
The delightful trail continues under a
canopy of trees, through a substantial
arched stone tunnel through a rock
outcrop, before passing through a
bridge arch to a final bridge over the
burn. This brings you directly to the
huge edifice of Falkland House, built
in 1844 by the Bruce family, and now
a school for boys with special needs.

The paths, bridges and tunnel
you have just walked are all part of
Falkland Estate, which used to be the
sporting playground of Stuart kings
and queens – also much loved by
Mary Queen of Scots.

At the next fork, either branch
brings you out onto a tarmac lane
where you turn right to walk down a
fine avenue of trees, past the Falkland
Estate car park and back to the village
by West Port. Falkland Palace, on
the east side of the High Street, is
brimming with history and should
not be missed, but your first port
of call may well be one of the many
local taverns – there are some good
tearooms too!

19. BISHOP HILL (461M/1,512FT)

MAP	OS SHEET 58 (GR 185044)
DISTANCE	10KM
ASCENT	310M
TIME	2.5–3.5 HRS
ACCESS	DESCRIBED ROUTE: BISHOP TERRACE CAR PARK, KINNESSWOOD (GR 178029) · GLEN VALE CAR PARK (GR 173069) · SCOTLANDWELL (GR 184017)
	GRADUAL ASCENT: HULL RESERVOIR CAR PARK (GR 225035)
DIFFICULTY	FAIRLY STEEP ASCENT ON A GRASSY PATH – EASIER OPTIONS AVAILABLE
SUMMARY	Bishop Hill strikes a grand, craggy profile above Loch Leven and the rolling farmland surrounding it. Not as popular as either East or West Lomond, Bishop Hill nevertheless deserves attention, not least for its dramatic pinnacled oddity known as Carlin Maggie, the Lomonds' most famous landmark.

BISHOP HILL IS the highest point of the steep, craggy escarpment to the north-east of Loch Leven. It is often combined with West Lomond, to the north, using the Glen Vale approach or by a circular tour from Holl reservoir. The described route is a fine little circular tour from the village of Kinnesswood and initially involves a steep, grassy ascent onto the top of the escarpment. If your preference is for a gradual, less steep walk, then the eastern approach from Holl Reservoir is recommended, but it can be quite boggy in places. The approach from Glen Vale is quite scenic and is described in Route 17 – West Lomond.

It should first be noted that the path shown on the map, ascending the escarpment from Easter Balgedie, can no longer be accessed from there, as the farmer at Balneathal Farm, from where the path starts, has seen fit to claim there are health and safety issues and has erected a notice to this effect. This is a fine, well-constructed path, however, and can still be reached from Kinnesswood if so desired.

In Kinnesswood, drive east up Bruce Road, which is situated at the south of the village. There is a car park on the left further up, off Bishop Terrace, a continuation of Bruce Road.

Walk up the road and go through the small gate to a grassy path which ascends to the right of a building and radio mast. Almost immediately, the path begins to go up the steep hillside and the passage of endless feet is obvious. Reach a narrow, flatter area with a path contouring along the hillside. A sign says this path is the Michael Bruce Way and offers the possibility of reaching the Easter Balgedie path by going left.

Michael Bruce was a local Kinnesswood gentleman, born in 1746, who soon earned the title 'the gentle poet of Loch Leven' for his numerous outpourings of well-crafted poems, ballads and songs describing the natural surroundings. Tragically he died aged only 21 from TB, which makes his prolific literary output all the more

incredible. You can learn more about him and see some of his poetry on a plaque in the village on your return.

Unless you have opted for going left continue upwards with no respite to the prominent line of dolerite crags directly above. Take any one of numerous grassy paths which find easy passages through the outcrop, or swing right to avoid them altogether.

Have a well-earned breather at the crest of the escarpment and admire the fine vista of Loch Leven and the distant Ochil Hills. Nearby is the Scottish Gliding Club's headquarters and on a windy day you are sure to see many gliders using the upcurrents to perform their graceful aerial manoeuvres. It is also a favourite spot for hang-gliders and para-gliders. High above, invisible skylarks will no

Bishop Hill from Benarty Hill viewpoint

doubt be warbling their symphony of song.

The actual summit is still 1km north of here and reached easily by following the crest of the ridge. There is a small, but prominent, cairn on the knoll which marks the summit.

To visit Carlin Maggie, descend west from the summit and cross the fence where you can drop down to the left of a line of steep dolerite crags. You will soon spot the 12m-high rock stack off to the right at the base of the crags. 'Carlin' is an old Scots word for witch and legend has it that Maggie had the temerity to challenge even the Devil's authority. Her punishment was to be struck by lightning as she fled across the hillside, turning her to stone for all eternity.

Return to the top of the escarpment and continue north along its crest on a good, undulating, grassy path, eventually following the line of an old dry stone wall. After about 1km of pleasant walking, begin the descent into the head of Glen Vale – the Covenanters' Glen. See the West Lomond walk description (Route 17) for more on this.

At the bottom, go over a gate on the left into a grassy field and follow a vague, grassy path southward, which subsequently keeps to the left of a fence at the lower part of the field. About 300m past a radio mast on the right, go through a gate and turn right down a rough vehicle track. At the next field, stay immediately to the right of a fence and dry stone wall and reach a minor road, where you turn left.

The road soon swings to the right, but keep straight on here along a track signposted to Springfield Farm. Go through a gate and then another to reach a path between two fences and walls. This soon leads to a wide farm track leading to the main road at Easter Balgedie. Turn left and follow the pavement for 1km to Kinnesswood and the starting point. The plaque about Michael Bruce, also giving other interesting village facts, is opposite the petrol station on the left-hand side.

Carlin Craig

20. BENARTY HILL ARTHUR'S HILL (356M/1,168FT)

MAP	OS SHEET 58 (GR 153979)
DISTANCE	6KM
ASCENT	230M
TIME	1.5–2 HRS
ACCESS	VANE FARM NATURE RESERVE CAR PARK (GR 160990)
DIFFICULTY	WELL-DEFINED PATH INITIALLY, LESS SO NEAR SUMMIT
SUMMARY	This fine wee hill rises dramatically above the south shore of Loch Leven and its rocky northern escarpment is a prominent feature when viewed from the M90 driving south.

BENARTY, THE MOST southerly of the Lomond Hills, stands in splendid isolation above the placid waters of Scotland's largest Lowland loch, Loch Leven, which has international importance as a birdwatcher's paradise: the loch is home to more breeding ducks than anywhere else in inland Europe and thousands of other birds use it as a winter stopover.

To reach the Vane Farm Reserve, turn off the M90 on the B9097 heading east and drive for about 2 miles before turning right into the large car park. Walk through the visitor centre outdoor section and turn right to reach an open, grassy area. Walk straight on and follow the sign saying 'Viewpoint Loop'.

The well-established trail makes a rising eastward traverse before hairpinning back upwards through birch woodland.

Just beyond a bench, take a left-hand fork and continue upwards,

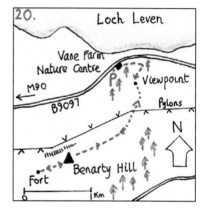

eventually reaching the fine viewpoint with a substantial cairn on a level promontory. Enjoy fine views of Loch Leven with its grassy island of St Serf's, a key breeding ground for birds. The priory on the island is now a ruin but was home to Augustinian monks in the 9th century.

Castle Island to the north-west was the ill-famed venue for the incarceration of Mary Queen of

On Benarty Hill

Scots, who was held captive there for a year until her daring escape in 1568. The steep slopes of Bishop Hill to the north-east make a pleasing backdrop to the loch.

For those who have climbed enough, the viewpoint loop walk can be continued by staying on the main trail. To continue to Benarty Hill, you will need to leave the obvious path. Head south, following a faint path running to the right of a fence and, later on, a dry stone dyke. Reach the corner of a field just next to an obvious pylon and cross the low wall into an adjacent field. A faint path to the right follows the dry stone wall past some curious hollows which are not natural but the result of quarrying. Cross the field, heading for

a group of prominent Scots Pines just to the left of some crags.

Climb directly upwards from here, gradually moving out to the right until you reach a fence that follows the line of the summit ridge. Cross the fence and reach a good, grassy path which heads south-west through heather, parallel to the fence and dyke. From here, it is less than a mile to the summit marked by a trig point.

For good views of the loch and summit it is a good idea to continue along the ridge path, descending to a dip, then climbing up the ridge beyond where there are remains of an Iron Age fort.

At the dip it is possible to cross the dyke and descend a steep grassy slope northwards where there is a good

Near the summit of Benarty Hill

view of the imposing dolerite crags below the ridge-line. This forms the start of a possible alternative route of return, but the terrain is pathless and tussocky, and not recommended – far easier to retrace the route of ascent, perhaps completing the other section of the viewpoint loop to finish.

21. LARGO LAW (290M/952FT)

MAP	OS SHEET 59 (GR 427050)
DISTANCE	3 KM
ASCENT	240M
TIME	1–2 HRS
ACCESS	CEMETERY CAR PARK, UPPER LARGO (GR 424037)
DIFFICULTY	EASY GRASS PATH WITH ONE SMALL, STEEP SECTION
SUMMARY	The steep-sided, grassy volcanic plug of Largo Law is a distinctive landmark from many parts of Fife and aside from the Lomond Hills 10 miles further west, it is the highest point in Fife. It stands guard over the curving sweep of Largo Bay on the Firth of Forth and its proximity to the sea gives it a commanding presence.

DESPITE ITS LOWLY stature (not even making 1,000ft), Largo Law is a worthwhile objective if only to gain an appreciation of the coastline and general topography of the East Fife landscape.

The Fife Coastal Path follows the curve of Largo Bay through the village of Lower Largo, famous for its connection with Alexander Selkirk, a sea lover who was stranded on a Pacific island for five years and provided the inspiration for Daniel Defoe's novel *Robinson Crusoe*. You can see a statue of him in the village.

The starting point for the walk up Largo Law is in the smaller village of Upper Largo, about 1km north-east of Lower Largo on the A917. Take the minor road left just before the junction of the A917 and the A915. The cemetery car park is about 300m up this road on the right-

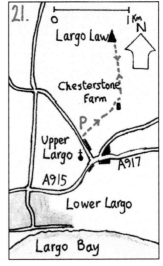

hand side next to a primary school.

A well-established grassy path leads in less than 1km to Chesterstone Farm. Follow the signed route

Largo Law

through the farm area and a gate at the back. Pass a small wind turbine before climbing steeply, directly up the hill, through clumps of gorse bushes. This path can be quite muddy in places, especially after heavy rain, and care should be taken.

Reach the little knoll of the south summit before dropping into a grassy dip and making a short ascent to the main top of Largo Law, which is crowned by a trig point and cairn about 20m apart. On a clear day, over the wide expanse of the Firth of Forth to the south, you should spot the cone of North Berwick Law and the Bass Rock to its left, both about 15 miles away. To the west, the Lomond Hills are generally visible across the flat lands of the Kingdom of Fife. The small, craggy eminence to the east is Craig Rock, another volcanic plug. Both Largo Law and Craig Rock were formed over 300 million years ago.

There is no practicable circular route on this hill and you should retrace your steps to return to the car park.

22. NORMAN'S LAW (285M/935FT)

MAP	OS SHEET 59 (GR 305203)
DISTANCE	5KM
ASCENT	230M
TIME	1.5–2 HRS
ACCESS	AYTON SMIDDY ON A913 NEWBURGH–CUPAR ROAD (GR 302180)
DIFFICULTY	EASY ASCENT ON VAGUE, GRASSY PATHS

Summary   Norman's Law is the highest of a number of small hills lining the south side of the Firth of Tay. Its fine, airy summit is dotted with crags and commands glorious views across the Tay Estuary to Dundee and northwards to the Sidlaws.

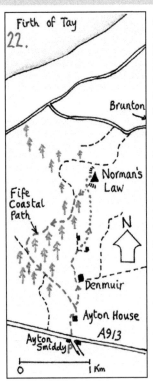

THE SHORTEST ROUTE to this hill is from the north, off the minor road west of the village of Brunton. However, a more interesting circular route from the south is described here. Park just off the A913 Newburgh to Cupar road on a minor road just past Ayton Smiddy. This road has a wide area near the fence with room for parking.

Walk up the vehicle track opposite, heading north directly towards the distinctive knoll of Norman's Law. Pass Ayton House on the right and go right at a fork just beyond at a signpost. You will pass a cottage on the

right with a large metal water wheel. This is the home of metal-worker Mike Robertson, who also made the metal direction indicator on the summit.

Continue straight on at Denmuir, passing a small pond, until you reach a gate with an arrow between two other gates to two private houses. Go through the middle gate and follow an intermittent path up the grassy hillside between gorse bushes. Avoid a little false summit by skirting round its right and follow a fence upwards by a wood until you are below a crag on the

Norman's Law

right. A variety of easy, grassy paths take you up to the summit where there is a small cairn, trig point and direction indicator.

On a fine day, the view north-east over the Firth of Tay to Dundee is marvellous, as are the views south-west to the twin cones of East and West Lomond.

To continue the circuit, descend back west to the edge of the wood and follow it downwards until you reach a log gate. Go through the gate and turn left at the track junction ahead. This is part of the Fife Coastal Path extension which has been rerouted to avoid private land. Stay on the track as it descends through the forest, passing Ayton Hill on the right before swinging left on a long, straight section which takes you back to Ayton House and the A913.

23. MONCREIFFE HILL (223M/732FT)

MAP	OS SHEET 58 (GR 136199)

FROM SOUTH-EAST CAR PARK:

DISTANCE	5KM
ASCENT	200M
TIME	1.5–2 HRS

FROM NORTH CAR PARK:

DISTANCE	2.5KM
ASCENT	150M
TIME	0.5–1 HR
ACCESS	SOUTH-EAST CAR PARK (GR 154193) · NORTH CAR PARK (GR 138209)
DIFFICULTY	EASY GOING ON EXCELLENT PATHS
SUMMARY	Like Kinnoull Hill 3km to the north, Moncreiffe Hill is one of Perth's beautiful, tree-bound viewpoints, forming a highly distinctive wooded and craggy ridge, well seen from the M90 on the approach to Perth from the south.

MONCREIFFE HILL IS a deservedly popular little hill, standing south of the River Tay and giving a superb view of the city of Perth. Its name derives from the Gaelic '*monadh craobh*' – 'hill of the tree' – which implies that natural woodland has

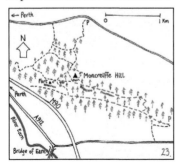

covered the slopes of the hill for a long time. The Woodland Trust bought the wood in 1988 and in 2010 secured more land north of the hill, creating a new car park and better woodland trails.

Although the north car park offers the quickest ascent of the hill, an ascent from the south-east car park gives a better appreciation of the long wooded ridge and superb views out over the Earn Valley to the Ochils and the Lomond Hills. A more satisfying circular walk can also be made from this car park and this is given in the description. It should be noted that there is over 14km of woodland trail on and around the hill, so further exploration would be well repaid.

Both car parks can be accessed by a loop road via the hamlet of Rhynd. This road goes round the eastern side of the hill, starting and finishing on the A912 from Bridge of Earn to Perth. To reach the south-east car park, turn right after crossing the bridge at the north end of Bridge of Earn, signposted to Rhynd and Elcho Castle. After about a mile, take a left turn signposted to Moncreiffe Hill to reach the fairly small car park, which is on a slope.

From the car park, follow the track west after going through a gate and take a right turn after 500m. This zigzags upwards through the trees before turning west to contour along the steep, wooded slopes of the south flank of the hill. This

is a marvellous high level promenade with a chance to appreciate the variety of trees such as Douglas Fir, Scots Pine, ash, oak and sycamore. At one point there is a seat at an open area with a bird's-eye view of the Earn Valley backed by the low, eastern end of the Ochils beyond.

After about 1.5km on this contouring traverse take a path forking off to the right leading to an information board in about 200m. Another, smaller path branches off to the right here to spiral round to the summit of Moncreiffe Hill known as Moredun Top. Moredun literally means 'big fort' and is the site of an Iron Age fort built by the Picts over 2,000 years ago. It is thought to have been the location of a battle in

On Moncreiffe Hill

Perth from Moncreiffe Hill

728AD between the Pictish warlords Angus and Alpin for control of the Pictish throne.

Enjoy the glorious view over Perth, with Kinnoull Hill on the right. In winter conditions the line of mountains forming the Highland Edge beyond is like a breaking wave.

Retrace your steps to the main traverse path and turn right 200m before taking some steps up to the left to visit a subsidiary top crowned by a trig point. This knoll was the site of another Iron Age hill fort and commands breathtaking views over the M90 to Bridge of Earn and beyond.

Return down the steps and turn right before going right again down a long flight of wooden steps to reach a wide vehicle track. Turn left here and follow this for around 2km back to the car park.

24. KINNOULL HILL (222M/728FT)

MAP	OS SHEET 53 OR 58 (GR 137228)

FROM PERTH – DESCRIBED ROUTE:

DISTANCE	5KM
ASCENT	220M
TIME	2–3 HRS

FROM CORSIEHILL OR QUARRY CAR PARK:

DISTANCE	2KM
ASCENT	110M
TIME	0.5–1 HR

FROM JUBILEE CAR PARK:

DISTANCE	3KM
ASCENT	80M
TIME	0.5–1 HR
ACCESS	PERTH SOUTH INCH CAR PARK (GR 120230) · CORSIEHILL OR QUARRY CAR PARK (GR 137237) · JUBILEE CAR PARK (GR 145237)
DIFFICULTY	EASY GOING ON EXCELLENT PATHS
SUMMARY	Kinnoull Hill, with its distinctive tower standing atop a craggy cliff edge and fine woodland trails, gives unrivalled views of the city of Perth, the Highlands, the Lomond Hills and the Tay Estuary. It is ideal for a short outing while in the Perth area.

KINNOULL HILL WOODLAND PARK was officially recognised as Scotland's first woodland park in 1991 and the rich diversity of trees, abundant wildlife and numerous trails have made it a popular destination, both for locals and visitors. It is unlikely that the walker will make a bee-line for the summit of the hill and return the same way, as there are many opportunities to create circular walks with three separate main access points to the hill. All routes are well signposted, but the route from the South Inch in Perth is

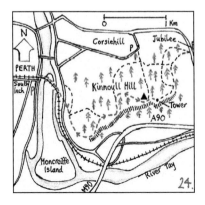

Kinnoull Hill

described here.

From the South Inch car park, the wooded slopes of Kinnoull Hill are very evident across the River Tay. Head directly to Tay Street (by the river) and go left until you reach the railway bridge crossing the river. Go up a flight of stone steps leading to a metal walkway which crosses the Tay, running parallel to the railway line. You will pass a sign indicating King James VI Golf Club on Moncreiffe Island. Turn right at the end of the bridge then left up a narrow alley and wide steps to the main road. Turn right and cross the road to the entrance to Branklyn Gardens. Head uphill here and follow the Kinnoull Hill signs. At a crossroads turn right (going straight on also goes to

Kinnoull Hill but you can return this way). Further on, take a left fork for a short distance and follow the path through the trees and eventually to the summit. En route, you will notice several minor paths branching off, all of which arrive at the top.

On the summit is a view indicator. The panorama of Highland hills to the north is a visual reminder of Perth and Kinnoull Hill being on the Highland Line, which separates the Highlands from the Central Belt. To the south and east, the Ochils and Lomond Hills are prominent, while directly across the Tay is Perth's other local hill – Moncreiffe Hill.

A walk up Kinnoull Hill is not complete without a visit to the round tower, or folly, standing proud on the

River Tay from Kinnoull Hill

edge of the steep, rocky escarpment a few hundred metres further on. The tower was built by the Earl of Kinnoull in the 18th century and was intended to be similar to the defensive structures seen high above German rivers such as the Rhine. On the approach, there are one or two superb vantage points where you can enjoy views of the tower and the mighty River Tay meandering eastward to distant Dundee.

Return to Perth is essentially by the route of ascent, but those with more time and energy will probably want to explore the many well-signposted woodland trails.

For those with cars (and less energy!), shorter walks to the summit can be made from Corsiehill and Jubilee car parks (see Information Box).

25. BIRNAM HILL (404M/1,325 FT)

MAP	OS SHEET 52 OR 53 (GR 032402)
DISTANCE	7KM
ASCENT	300M
TIME	2–3 HRS
ACCESS	DUNKELD RAILWAY STATION · BIRNAM HOTEL (GR 031417)
DIFFICULTY	GOOD PATHS WITH INITIAL STEEP SECTION
SUMMARY	A beautiful wooded hill with ancient associations with Shakespeare's *Macbeth*, Birnam Hill straddles the edge of the Highlands and offers glorious vistas in all directions. The described route is a fine, circular, well-signposted leg-stretcher.

BIRNAM HILL OCCUPIES a prime position on the geological edge of the Highlands, rising high above Birnam and Dunkeld, the two pretty villages marking the gateway to Highland Perthshire.

The easiest starting point for the circuit is at Dunkeld railway station adjacent to the A9, where there is plenty of room for parking. Alternatively, you may wish to park in Birnam village near the station and begin at the signpost opposite Birnam Hotel.

At the north end of the station, go down some wide steps and turn left under the railway, staying on the footpath to the left. Reach a tarmac lane with a signpost indicating two routes to Birnam Hill. Take the one going directly

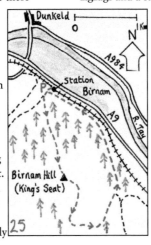

ahead, which is also marked Inchewan (the route indicating Birnam Hill to the left is your return route). About 100m after this signpost, turn sharp left at another signpost for Birnam Hill. From here, the path climbs fairly steeply through natural forest of mainly broad-leaf trees. After several zigzags and a stretch of more open terrain, there is a grand view of Birnam and Dunkeld. This view is best appreciated from a craggy bluff just to the left of the path, where you can rest and enjoy the marvellous bird's-eye panorama of Dunkeld, the Tay, distant Deuchary Hill and the Beinn a'Ghlo massif beyond. This is one of the finest viewpoints in Perthshire.

Birnam and Dunkeld from Birnam Hill

Beyond this viewpoint the path levels off somewhat, meandering its way pleasantly through Scots Pine before the final steep little pull up the heathery dome of the summit, which is crowned with a huge cairn. The cairn even has its own set of stone steps leading to the flat top.

The difference in character between Highlands and Lowlands can be greatly appreciated from the summit cairn. To the south, the sprawling patchwork of fields and woods contrasts greatly with the grand Munros of Highland Perthshire to the north, including the conical Schiehallion and Ben Vrackie. The windfarm to the left of Schiehallion is the only blot on a marvellous panorama. The prominent little hill about 2km to the south-west (marked on the OS map as the Obney Hills) has a summit trig point and the scattered remains of an old fort. An extra excursion to visit this hill is easily attainable for those with unlimited energy and time.

To continue the circuit, follow the signpost indicating Quarry car park and go over a small rise before descending steeply down a wide gully on a well-constructed set of wooden steps to a flat area with a couple of stone seats – another grand viewpoint. From here, the path swings right then left in a huge arc before passing the signpost for Stair Bridge viewpoint, a short distance off to the right.

Continue north-eastwards on the main trail as it descends gradually

Birnam Hill

through forest, ignoring any side trails forking off to the left or right. You will gradually become aware of the noise of traffic on the A9 as you lose height. At the bottom of the hill turn left and follow the signs to Dunkeld, firstly on a vehicle track then on a meandering walking trail through woods, before finally meeting a lane taking you to the junction near the station mentioned at the beginning of the route description.

26. DEUCHARY HILL (511M/1,676FT)

MAP	OS SHEET 52 OR 53 (GR 037485)
DISTANCE	15KM
ASCENT	400M
TIME	4–5 HRS
ACCESS	CALLY CAR PARK, NORTH OF DUNKELD (GR 024437)
DIFFICULTY	MAINLY EXCELLENT VEHICLE TRACKS WITH STEEP PATH TO SUMMIT
SUMMARY	A fairly secluded hill of immense character and unique charm set amongst the delightfully wooded and wild, loch-sprinkled countryside north of Dunkeld. This is a hill to savour and enjoy at leisure, exploring the many lochs which surround the peak.

NORTH OF DUNKELD lies over 150 square km of beautiful, wooded hill country peppered with idyllic lochans, the largest of these being Loch Ordie, a popular walking objective and for many the jewel in the crown of this enticing area. Just south of Loch Ordie stands Deuchary Hill, a 'single malt' of a hill which will repay in full repeated visits – I speak from experience.

Although there are shorter approaches, the most scenic is from the south, beginning at the Cally car park just north of Dunkeld. To reach this, drive north through Dunkeld on the A923. Just past a sharp bend to the

right, drive left up the bumpy lane signposted to the car park, about 300m on the left.

From the car park, take the wooded trail north, signposted to Mill Dam and Loch Ordie, past Upper Hatton. The trail here is on a well-maintained vehicle track meandering through woods and open ground with fine views ahead. At the Glack Kennels, go through a metal gate and reach Mill Dam, an idyllic little lochan with its own pair of swans. Take the minor path to the right, which passes the dam at the southern end of the lochan and continues on and gradually upwards,

Deuchary Hill

giving delightful views across the water. After 1km, reach a path junction just beyond a stone bridge. Take the right-hand path and watch out for boggy terrain as it winds its way upwards through stands of stunted Scots Pine. After almost 1km the path makes a sharp turn to the right, crossing a small stream. About 50m beyond the bend, another little path should be visible, forking off to the left near a large boulder. This leads to the summit of Deuchary Hill in only 0.5km with one short steep section.

The summit trig point at 509m is actually 2m lower than the true summit, which is formed by a sharp fin of mica-schist rock with an obvious white quartzite intrusion. The base of this makes an excellent back-rest for an extended summit fester! Enjoy the fine view north and west to tranquil Loch Ordie with the cone of Schiehallion very obvious.

Descent can be by the route of ascent but the advised and described route descends north-west from the summit on an intermittent path which passes the east side of beautiful Lochan na Beinne, a charming little hill loch just below the summit. A more obvious path continues on from here meandering its way down to Loch Ordie at Lochordie Lodge. Loch Ordie is a marvellous spot to rest for a while and absorb the peace and tranquillity of this unique area.

There are two possible return routes to your starting point. The slightly

The summit of Deuchary Hill

quicker route, on the upper Loch Ordie Trail, includes part of the same path just used to reach the loch. It swings in a wide arc round the western flank of Deuchary Hill and after about 3km reaches the path junction near the stone bridge mentioned on the outward route. Alternatively, take the lower Loch Ordie Trail, which begins 300m north-west of Lochordie Lodge at a bridge over the loch outflow burn. This route is on a vehicle track descending in 2.5km to Raor Lodge before going through a gate on the left and passing two additional lochs (Dowally and Rotmell), finally reaching Mill Dam and the outward route.

27. LAMMER LAW (527M/1,729FT)

MAP	OS SHEET 66 (GR 523618)
DISTANCE	12KM
ASCENT	350M
TIME	3.5–4.5 HRS
ACCESS	DESCRIBED CIRCULAR ROUTE: WEST HOPES ROAD END (GR 557633)
	DIRECT ROUTE: LAMMER LAW ROAD END (GR 538637)
DIFFICULTY	WELL-DEFINED TRACKS AND PATHS
SUMMARY	Lammer Law is the second highest of the Lammermuir hills and the shapeliest and most distinctive of the range. It is also the best viewpoint. If you only ever climb one hill in the Lammermuirs, then this is the one to do!

THE LAMMERMUIRS (lammer moors) are the Southern Uplands' most north-easterly hill range and are essentially a wild, windswept and lonely moorland plateau that receives few visitors. In some respects the Lammermoors are southern Scotland's equivalent to the Monadhliath range in the Highlands, another high, rolling plateau with few distinct summits. On a positive note, heather moorland is a globally rare habitat, of which three-quarters occurs in the UK and the majority of that in Scotland. The Lammermuirs are a prime example of this unique habitat and

an important strand of our natural heritage. The area provided inspiration for Sir Walter Scott's romantic novel *The Bride of the Lammermoors*.

For those hardened high-pointers (and Marilyn-baggers!) who must climb Meikle Says Law, (the Lammermuirs' high point at 535m) it is possible to combine this with Lammer Law in a single walk. The 8km walk between the two is pure Lammermuir, mostly trackless tussock and bog – a navigational nightmare in mist. Even in clear conditions this is not a gentle stroll. Note that Meikle Says Law lies far to

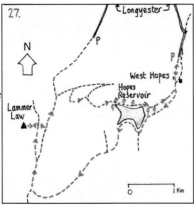

En route to Lammer Law

the east of Lammer Law and is on OS map 67.

The second time I climbed Lammer Law, I did not include the featureless and viewless 'Meikle' and discovered a fine circular tour, described here. Park at the end of the public road, between East Hopes and West Hopes, where there is a large parking area on the left. The village of Gifford lies about 5 miles to the north, which itself lies south of Haddington, just off the A1.

Walk south along the vehicle track past West Hopes Farm and at a gate take the middle of three tracks, which contours along the lower slopes above Hopes Water. Note that the left-hand track climbing steeply up the obvious heathery spur is not shown on some maps, nor are several others in the area.

As you head along the track, the well-landscaped grassy embankment of the Hopes Reservoir Dam comes into view and the gentle slopes of Bleak Law rise up beyond the reservoir, with the summit of Lammer Law, not yet visible, beyond. The track meanders round the south side of the reservoir and into a minor glen below the slopes of Bleak Law. Ignore a track branching off to the right and continue along the main track, as it leaves the minor glen to climb an obvious spur onto the plateau above. This track is also unmarked on earlier maps. On the plateau it meets another track coming in from the south.

Turn right here to follow the track

The summit of Lammer Law

north, ignoring a right-hand fork further on. The summit of Lammer Law should now be visible to the left. Stay on the track until you are immediately east of the summit, where you follow a path on the left for 300m to the top.

The summit has a fairly large cairn, possibly a burial cairn or remains of a small fort – its antiquity is unquestionable, and it is marked as such on the map. There is also a trig point. The finest view is to the north, with the landmarks of Bass Rock, North Berwick Law and Traprain Law, and the green patchwork of the Lothian plain.

Return to the main track and go through a gate opposite. Follow a vague path heading roughly

south-east, or aim directly for the disturbingly intrusive windfarm on the horizon, until you reach another track roughly parallel to the one you were on. This is the track shown on the map and is a very old right of way, running from Gifford to Carfraemill via Longyester. It also forms the direct route to the summit mentioned above.

Turn left on this track and follow it along one of many of Lammer Law's northern spurs. Where the fence ends on the right, after about 1km, turn right, to follow another fence down to a grassy col. Hopes Reservoir is visible off to the right from here. Climb the fence and descend for a few hundred metres to meet another grassy track, where you turn right into a secluded, grassy hollow by the Sting Bank Burn. Cross the burn and follow this (unmarked) track as it meanders round the spurs of Bleak Law to the western end of the reservoir.

The best, and the quickest, route from here is to follow the northern side of the reservoir by a pleasant little path through a birchwood. This path can be reached via a gate, visible just above the reservoir. Reach the dam after 1km and follow the main track as it zigzags down through more woodland, crossing the Hopes Water to follow its southern bank northwards back to West Hopes and your starting point.

28. DIRRINGTON GREAT LAW (398M/1,307FT)

MAP	OS SHEET 67 (GR 698549)
DISTANCE	4KM
ASCENT	200M
TIME	1–1.5 HRS
ACCESS	BRIDGE OVER BLACKSMILL BURN ON THE LONGFORMACUS–DUNS ROAD (GR 705560)
DIFFICULTY	ILL-DEFINED, BOGGY PATH
SUMMARY	Dirrington Great Law and its southerly sister, Dirrington Little Law, both volcanic remnants, are two distinctive eastern outliers of the sprawling Lammermuirs, and have shapely profiles. The following route description describes the ascent of Great Law only, but can be extended to include both.

DIRRINGTON GREAT LAW is less than 3km south of the Southern Upland Way (SUW) long-distance route across Scotland and could easily be included in an 'off day' if you are staying at Longformacus, which lies on the SUW.

Note that the straight path indicated on the OS map, starting at GR 697567, from the minor road into Longformacus, is virtually non-existent, and although the map gives the impression of a good approach route to the hill, is certainly no such thing. The best approach is from the bridge over the Blacksmill Burn, 1km further on, past a long avenue of trees. This is less than 2km from Longformacus. There is limited parking near the end of the line of birch trees.

Go through the gate by the bridge and follow a grassy path south-westwards by the edge of the field. This gradually swings left higher up to meet another path coming from the farm at Dronshiel. Go left onto this second path, which contours along the base of the hill. There are several ruins of old shielings scattered about this area. Reach a third path going through deep heather and grassy tussocks directly up the north-eastern slopes. Towards the top, the path swings right then doubles back to the flat summit, where twin cairns flank a collapsed trig point. The cairns, originally Iron Age burial mounds, are now worn down substantially.

There is a similar cairn on the top of

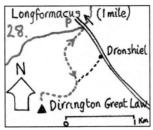

Dirrington Great Law

Dirrington Little Law, 2km to the south-west and if you also wish to climb this hill, add another hour and a half to the estimated time given in the Information Box. The best approach is to adopt a more or less direct line via remote Kippetlaw, though the going is tough and relatively pathless. It would be easier to climb this hill separately from the B6456, south of the hill.

Return from Dirrington Great Law by the route of ascent, or alternatively via Dronshiel and the road.

29. BROUGHTON HEIGHTS (571M/1,874FT)

MAP	OS SHEET 72 (GR 123411)
DISTANCE	11KM
ASCENT	500M
TIME	3–5 HRS
ACCESS	BROUGHTON PLACE CAR PARK (GR 119374)
DIFFICULTY	GOOD TRACKS AND WELL-DEFINED RIDGE PATH
SUMMARY	The compact and distinct range of hills known as the Broughton Heights lies between Peebles and Biggar and is a popular walkers' destination. The range is named after the highest point (Broughton Heights), a grand viewpoint on the north of the group. The most southern top of Trahenna Hill is a distinctive hill in its own right and the traverse between the two, described here, is a wonderful, high-level ridge walk.

THE JOHN BUCHAN WAY (JBW), a relatively recent addition to Scotland's growing collection of waymarked trails, is a 21km route from Peebles to the picturesque hamlet of Broughton and part of this route is used to access these hills. John Buchan spent many long summer holidays with his grandparents in Broughton and gradually grew to love the surrounding hills and woods on his walks and rambles. The knowledge and enjoyment gleaned from his wanderings subsequently became the inspiration for many of his later novels, particularly *The Thirty-Nine Steps*.

About 1km north of Broughton on the A701, turn off east along a minor road signposted to Broughton Place. The walkers' car park lies 1km on, past several houses. Go through a gate on the JBW and turn right almost immediately onto an intermittent, grassy path which ascends one of the many north-western spurs of Trahenna Hill. This leads quickly onto the broad south-west ridge, where there is a fence and path. Follow the path by the fence along the crest of the ridge until you reach a fence junction. The summit of Trahenna

On the ridge looking to Broughton Heights

Hill, on an outlying spur, can be reached by a short detour of a few hundred metres, by first climbing the fence and then following the other fence. A few stones and a wooden post mark the summit, a fine viewpoint.

Prominent to the south are the complex ridges and spurs of the Corbett, Dollar Law and its collection of satellite Donalds while to the west Culter Fell and Tinto dominate the view.

Your next objective, Broughton Heights, lies 4km to the north. Retrace your steps to the fence junction and turn right to follow an excellent grassy path next to a dry stone wall and fence. This gives fine, undulating ridge-walking over several minor tops, one, Point 498, having a cairn. From Hammer Head, the last top, descend steeply by a fine and heathery path to Hammer Head Pass, a broad, grassy col where you pick up the JBW. Turn left on the Way for a few hundred metres before forking

right to reach the pass between Clover Law on the left and Broomy Side on the right.

Ascend the south-west ridge of Broomy Side by an easy, grassy path and continue north over the broad summit of Green Law, the penultimate top before Broughton Heights, 1km onwards. Slap-bang on the Southern Uplands Boundary Fault line, Broughton Heights has a commanding position looking over the Lowland plain to the Pentlands and beyond. The actual Fault line makes a curious kink from here up to Penicuik, before doubling back to resume its north-easterly direction to Dunbar on the east coast.

Return by retracing your steps to the pass below Broomy Side, where you meet the JBW which is followed for 2.5km back to the car park by a pleasant, low-level route skirting the east flank of Clover Law. Those with energy to spare may wish to traverse Clover Law rather than follow the JBW.

30. EILDON NORTH HILL (404M/1,325FT)
31. EILDON MID HILL (422M/1,385FT)

MAP	OS SHEET 73 (GR 554328, 548323)
DISTANCE	9KM
ASCENT	410M
TIME	3–4 HRS
ACCESS	CAR PARK OPPOSITE MELROSE ABBEY (GR 547343)
DIFFICULTY	EASY GOING ON MAINLY EXCELLENT PATHS AND TRACKS
SUMMARY	The two main summits of the Eildon Hills stand proud and prominent to the south of Melrose and are without doubt the iconic Borders landmark, seen from all points of the compass. The hills are steeped in Border legend and history and provide a marvellous circular walk with incredible views.

THE EILDONS CONSIST of three distinct peaks, the two mentioned in the Information Box above, and a smaller one to the south, oddly named Eildon Wester. The described walk includes this third hill.

The name Eildon is a possible

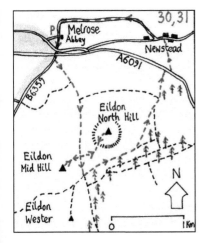

derivation from the old English '*eld dun*', meaning 'old fort', and indeed Eildon North Hill was once the site of a substantial Iron Age hill fort.

Geologically, the triple peaks are the remnants of a composite laccolith, whereby a mass of molten magma intruded into the surrounding underground sandstone. Following millions of years of erosion of the sandstone, the lava plugs were exposed to the surface to form the result we see today.

The fort on the North Hill was once a major tribal capital of a people known as the Selgovae. Within the ramparts of the fort, some 300 hut circles have been identified and it is estimated that the hill must have had a population of over 1,000 – far more than the number of present-day summit baggers on an Easter Sunday afternoon!

The Eildon Hills

The Romans took over Eildon North and demolished the fort, before erecting a signal station on the summit. They consolidated their hold on the area by creating a great camp at Trimontium (the place of the three hills) which was situated below the hills at what is now Newstead, the oldest inhabited village in Scotland. The described walk passes through this village.

Melrose is a bustling, tourist honey-pot in the summer months, but you should find room in the large car park opposite historic Melrose Abbey in the town centre. The abbey itself is arguably the finest of the Border abbeys. Its impressive ruins are definitely worth a visit, before or after your walk.

The 106km route known as St Cuthbert's Way connecting Melrose with the island of Lindisfarne in England is well signposted and can be followed for the first part of the route right up to the col between the two main Eildon Hills. This is also now part of the Scottish National Trail (SNT), the mammoth 756km route from Kirk Yetholm to Cape Wrath devised by Cameron McNeish.

Follow the St Cuthbert's Way sign south on the B6359, uphill, into the town square, where you then follow the signs saying 'Eildons Walk'. The route goes uphill for around 200m before turning left into a narrow alley between terraced houses. Go over a bridge, then up a huge flight of wooden steps. Follow an often

The view from Eildon Mid Hill

muddy path as it climbs upwards fairly steeply between fields and subsequently gorse bushes, to eventually reach the col between the two hills.

Turn left, to ascend by one of a number of paths, the grassy summit of Eildon North Hill. Still visible are the remains of the circular ditch which enclosed the Roman signal station.

Return to the col and follow the obvious path up Mid Hill, which is quite steep in the upper reaches and soon takes you to the trig point and viewpoint indicator. Owing to the Eildon Hills' position in the Tweed Valley, their relative height gives unimpeded views in all directions. First impressions are of a glorious,

green patchwork of fields and forests stretching in all directions. However, take time to 'stand and stare', or rather, sit and stare, and you should be able to pick out much detail. Far to the south-east, the long blue line of the Cheviots form a hazy horizon while directly south you should be able to pick out Rubers Law and the twin cones of the Minto Hills. The nearest higher ground is that of the Ettrick hills to the west.

Sir Walter Scott was greatly inspired by the Eildon Hills and surrounding country, and local tales of the supernatural and Border reivers fired his imagination. In 1812, he bought a farm 5km west of Melrose, demolished the original building and created a Gothic-style mansion:

Abbotsford. Here he wrote many of his famous novels and here he died in 1832. His burial place is in Dryburgh Abbey, just east of the Eildon Hills. The road to the abbey runs high above the Tweed, where there is a magnificent view of the Eildon Hills, supposedly the writer's favourite. 'Scott's View', as it is known, has an indicator plaque and is worth a visit.

There is a choice of routes from Mid Hill, depending on time, inclination and energy. The described route takes an easy contouring line round the south to Newstead and back to Melrose. For those who have had enough, simply return by the route of ascent. If you are keen to climb the third Eildon summit, descend west to a small stone shelter before dropping down to meet a good path running along the south of Mid Hill. Follow this eastwards and take the second path on the right, leading to the top of Eildon Wester (the south top). Retrace your steps to the main path and turn right to a path junction below the col between the main summits. From here, you can continue with the described route or make a quick return to Melrose by a short ascent to the col on a good path before retracing the route of ascent.

For those doing the described circular route, retrace your steps west to the col before turning right down a path to reach the path junction mentioned before. Go right for about 50m then left just before a metal gate. About 100m on, a metal gate on the right leads to a forest track which is followed eastwards to a clearing on the left. There is an Eildon Hills signpost here. Turn left on a muddy path to a large group of trees.

For a quicker return to Melrose, there is a path which contours back round the north flank of North Hill, leading to the original ascent path.

Stay on the rather muddy path which goes downhill past a recently built house on the left to the (now unused) A6091. Turn right then left after 100m, signposted with a three hills logo signpost. This takes you on a track down to Newstead, where you turn left then take the right fork a few hundred metres later (lower road). This leads back to Melrose and the abbey in about 1.5km.

32. RUBERS LAW (424M/1,391FT)

MAP	OS SHEET 80 (GR 580156)
DISTANCE	5KM
ASCENT	270M
TIME	1.5–2.5 HRS
ACCESS	WHITRIGGS, LIMITED PARKING (GR 561158)
DIFFICULTY	GENTLE ASCENT ON A VERY INDISTINCT GRASSY PATH
SUMMARY	Rising high above rolling farm country between Hawick and Jedburgh, the volcanic cone of Rubers Law, like the Eildon Hills further north, is a distinctive Borders landmark associated with a rich history.

Dark Ruberslaw, that lifts his head sublime
Rugged and hoary with the wrecks of time
On his broad misty front the giant wears
The horrid furrows of ten thousand years.

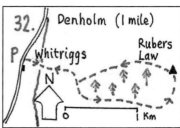

THE ABOVE LINES were written by John Leyden (1775–1811) who lived in the pretty village of Denholm, just north of the hill. Like Robert Burns, he was a learned scholar from 'peasant stock' and a contemporary of Sir Walter Scott.

The Borders Abbeys Way passes to the north of the hill and Rubers Law would make a worthwhile diversion for those tackling this long-distance route. There is no obvious route up this hill and various approaches are possible. The recommended route begins at Whitriggs to the west of the hill.

Parking near Whitriggs Farm is

On Rubers Law

The Eildon Hills from the summit of Rubers Law

limited, but the grass verge is wide enough to take a car. Follow a farm track heading east, with the rocky top of Rubers Law very prominent, directly ahead. Cross the stream and swing right then left up to the foot of a forestry plantation 1km from the start.

Follow the edge of the plantation to the right on a grassy path which climbs up to a dry stone wall. There is a gate in the dyke which, at the time of writing, was unusable so you may need to climb here. Follow a fence on a vague path through the heather up to the small knoll of the south summit. There is a gate here and a path leading north to the true summit, a fine rocky cone.

The steep, craggy summit area is partly natural and partly the remains of an Iron Age fort. West of the trig point there is a steep line of crags about 6m high, above a boulder and scree basin, forming part of the defensive ditch of the fort. In later times it is very likely that the fort was rebuilt and reused as a signal station by the Romans.

The views from the summit are extensive, with the twin cones of the Eildon Hills prominent 16km to the north. To the south-east the high mass of the Cheviots forms an undulating crest, but it is the infinite shades of foreground green expressed through the mosaic patchwork of rolling meadows and trees which really catches the eye.

Return by the same route or, alternatively, by descending west directly from the summit and following the northern boundary of the forestry plantation to meet up with the ascent path at the western end of the plantation.

33. MAIDEN PAPS (510M/1,673FT)

MAP	OS SHEET 79 (GR 500024)
DISTANCE	11KM
ASCENT	400M
TIME	4–6 HRS
ACCESS	B6399 – SUNDHOPE ROAD END (GR 517985)
DIFFICULTY	MAINLY ROUGH WALKING ON TUSSOCKY TERRAIN
SUMMARY	Like the Eildon Hills nearly 20 miles north, this shapely pair of hills are a distinctive Borders landmark, though less well-known. Their ascent, along with the bulkier Marilyn, Greatmoor Hill, makes a fine circuit.

THE APPROPRIATENESS OF the name (maiden breasts) given to this prominent pair is apparent from several viewpoints, but from others, only the higher of the two is visible. Do not confuse the pair with their far northern counterpart, the singular Maiden Pap in Caithness, another Hugh (see Route 96).

Unless you live in the Borders, Maiden Paps are a long way from anywhere and almost totally surrounded by Sitka Spruce plantations. They are best approached from the lonely B6399 road running south from Hawick and passing to the east of the pair. A good view of the Paps can be had from this road at the point where it is due east of them. This view looks west along a furrowed depression known as the Catrail, a strange linear earthwork possibly constructed in the Middle Ages as a defensive barrier, or possibly a

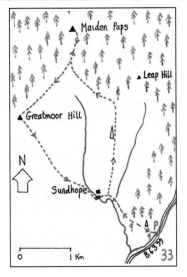

boundary marker, no-one really knows for sure. The Forestry Commission have left the ditch unplanted and it is now a glorified firebreak. Unless you have masochistic tendencies, it is best not to try and walk along it, as the

Maiden Paps

going is slow and tiring on a bed of soft vegetation and tussocks.

Further along this approach road you will pass Whitrope Heritage Centre, the high point of the old railway route from Edinburgh to Carlisle, now a walking centre. Beyond here, the road descends to the starting point of the walk, just before a sharp bend, where a track marked Sundhope goes off to the right. Parking is limited, but there is room for at least one car without blocking the entrance.

Walk along the track and through a gate at the forest edge, before descending to go through a second gate. Turn off the track just beyond a dry stone wall to ascend the broad grassy spur of Sundhope Rig (ridge), going through a gap in a dry stone wall higher up.

As you gain height, head directly towards a tall radio mast unmarked on earlier maps. Faint all terrain vehicle tracks exist up to and beyond this point, but the going can be quite slow on sphagnum moss and grassy tussocks, especially after heavy rain.

The grassy cone rising out of the trees directly ahead could be mistaken for the Paps, but is actually another volcanic plug named Leap Hill. At Black Rig, turn left to follow the forest edge for 1km, climbing steeply onto the summit of Scaw'd Law, where there is a fine view of the two Paps to the north.

Follow the ridge, cushions of soft heather and sphagnum moss making for fairly slow going. A final, steep, grassy ascent takes you to the small, airy summit of the highest Pap, a wonderful viewpoint. On a clear day the twin cones of the Eildon Hills and the distinctive Rubers Law stand out to the north, while the shapely Skelfhill Pen lies much closer, to the west. These are all Hughs. The smaller Pap can be reached in a few minutes by descending and crossing the bouldery defile between them.

Retrace your steps to Scaw'd Law, going through a gate in the fence beyond, before following the fence across a boggy flat col and up grassy slopes to the flat summit of Greatmoor Hill, crowned by a trig point and flattened cairn. This is another fine viewpoint.

Descend south-east from the summit on initially steep slopes, heading directly to Sundhope Burn and Farm. At the farm, cross the burn on a wooden bridge and regain the track used on the approach. Follow this back to your starting point.

34. SKELFHILL PEN (532M/1,745FT)

MAP	OS SHEET 79 (GR 441032)
DISTANCE	6KM
ASCENT	300M
TIME	2–3 HRS
ACCESS	QUARRY CAR PARK (GR 463050)
DIFFICULTY	GOOD TRACK FOLLOWED BY GRASSY PATHLESS ASCENT
SUMMARY	The unusually rocky cone of Skelfhill Pen is another Borders landmark offering wonderful views of the surrounding countryside.

THE SUFFIX '*PEN*' derives from the Cumbric (or old Welsh) language and, indeed, is the prefix of the names of many Welsh hills. In Scotland it has subsequently evolved to mean any hill with a striking profile, such as Ettrick Pen and Skelfhill Pen. The origin of Skelfhill is uncertain.

Lava flows from the Carboniferous Age are responsible for this hill and also Maiden Paps, Rubers Law and Dirrington Great Law.

The route starts near the farm of Skelfhill, which is reached by car taking the signposted Skelfhill road off the A7 Edinburgh to Carlisle road, 6 miles south-west of Hawick. Drive along this minor road for about 3 miles, before bearing right towards Skelfhill Farm. Park at a small disused quarry on the right where there is a sign indicating this is a car park.

Walk up the minor road towards the farm and fork right to go through the farmyard. From here, a track

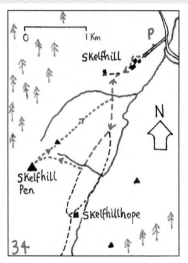

heads towards a cottage, where you veer right and then straight on past the rear of the cottage. Ignore another track that leads up the hill to Fouledge.

The hill seen directly ahead at this point is Grey Pen, the northerly subsidiary top of Skelfhill Pen.

The summit of Skelfhill Pen

Continue downhill and go through a couple of gates before reaching a fork in the track. Take the right fork, which gradually ascends the grassy, eastern flank of Skelfhill Pen.

After crossing a small stream, go through a gate and turn right off the track to follow a fence directly up the hillside. Higher up, a mildly rocky ridge gains height quickly to reach the narrow, grassy summit of Skelfhill Pen, crowned by a trig point and large cairn.

The extensive views include the rolling Border hills of Liddlesdale, Teviotdale and Eskdalemuir. The cone of Maiden Paps is very obvious to the east.

For those whose appetite has not yet been whetted, there is the option of completing a grand horseshoe of tops, including White Hill, Millstone Edge, Cauldcleuch Head (a Graham), Skelfhill Fell and Holywell Rig. Otherwise, continue north-east over Grey Pen and descend easy ground to reach the outward track by a metal gate. Note that there are numerous electric fences around here, so be careful and use gates where possible. Finally, follow the track back through Skelfhill Farm to the car park.

35. CRIFFEL (569M/1,868FT)

MAP	OS SHEET 84 (GR 957618)
DISTANCE	6KM
ASCENT	530M
TIME	2–3.5 HRS
ACCESS	ARDWALL CAR PARK SOUTH OF NEW ABBEY (GR 970634)
DIFFICULTY	WELL-DEFINED PATH, BOGGY IN THE UPPER REACHES
SUMMARY	The isolated and distinguished granite dome of Criffel, towering above the Nith estuary and Solway Firth, is an iconic landmark of the area. It is a popular walkers' destination with a well-trodden path to its summit, which unsurprisingly is a phenomenal viewpoint, perhaps the best in southern Scotland.

THE NAME 'CRIFFEL' appeared as 'Crafel' on 18th century maps and originates from the old Scots 'craw's fell' (crow's hill). Being a prominent landmark from the sea, the Vikings held the hill in high esteem and named it Kraka-fjell, translating as Raven's Hill, the raven being sacred in parts of Scandanavia. So, take your pick between crows or ravens!

Being the highest point for nearly 40km, and rising to almost 2,000ft, Criffel totally dominates the Solway Firth, the Galloway coastline and the farmland surrounding Dumfries. Other than the Lowther Hills far to the north, the next higher hills are those of the Lake District in England. Criffel is not on the radar of many hillwalkers, being fairly remote from Central Scotland and somewhat out on a limb, but on a clear day the views repay the effort handsomely.

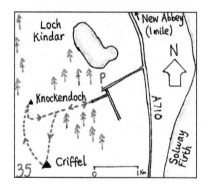

The described route is the popular one from the walkers' car park at Ardwall, but there are longer ones starting from the picturesque and historic village of New Abbey just to the north, definitely worth a visit. About 2 miles south of New Abbey on the A710, turn onto a minor road and track signposted 'Ardwall Mains'. At the end of the track, the car park is on the right.

Criffel

Go through a gate on the south side of the entrance track to follow a farm track for about 100m, before going right through another gate to a second farm track heading west to a forestry plantation. This is normally well signposted. Go through another gate and enter the forest on a good path, which soon enters a wide firebreak with the path going up the south side of the Craigrockall Burn.

The path takes an uncompromising, direct line up the eastern flank of the hill and despite the helpful granite steps in places it is difficult to adopt an efficient hillwalking rhythm. The granite bedrock seen at Criffel is also prevalent in other areas of the Southern Uplands, such as Cairnsmore of Fleet and the Dungeon Hills near Glen Trool.

Cross over two forestry tracks running at right angles to the path and continue upwards to reach the upper edge of the forestry plantation. Ignore a bridge over the burn on your right and keep directly ahead through a gap in the fence, where the path changes direction to follow an almost straight line directly to the summit. This steep and unrelenting final kilometre has been eroded by the passage of thousands of summit-fevered feet and can be a real mud-bath in places.

After 250m of vertical height, and no doubt a good dose of curses later, you will reach the large cairn and trig point marking the relatively flat summit of Criffel. On the map the cairn is named Douglas' Cairn and refers to the Earl of Douglas, a powerful earl of the Middle Ages who possibly used the hill as a lookout post in defending his land against the English.

The panorama from the summit on a clear day is unparalleled in the Southern Uplands and it is worth spending a good while devouring the views as well as your sandwiches. There is so much to see from the summit that it is difficult to know where to start. South and east across the watery expanse of the Solway Firth, the Lakeland mountains of England can clearly be seen. The only blot in this view is the thoroughly obtrusive forest of wind-turbines out to sea. To the south-west, the meandering line of the Galloway coast draws the eye and you should also spot the Isle of Man and the distant hills of Ireland. To the north lies the pretty village of New Abbey and, beyond, the urban sprawl of Dumfries.

Rather than just descend the same way, the route visits the little northern outlying top of Knockendoch. A fairly obvious path heads north-west from the summit on a broad, easy-angled ridge and swings round to the north for 1.5km to reach the top of Knockendoch, where there is another cairn. This is also a fine viewpoint where you can gain a retrospective view of Criffel.

To descend from here, retrace your steps for a few hundred metres to the lowest point between here and Criffel, then drop down eastwards on an easy grassy slope to the edge of the forest and the path of ascent. Follow this back to the car park.

36. SCREEL HILL (343M/1,125FT)

MAP	OS SHEET 84 (GR 780553)
DISTANCE	9KM
ASCENT	410M
TIME	3–4.5 HRS
ACCESS	SCREEL WOOD CAR PARK (GR 800547)
DIFFICULTY	MAINLY GOOD FOREST TRACKS AND PATHS
SUMMARY	Screel Hill is a deservedly popular walk on account of its rugged character and stunning view of the Solway coast. This walk combines Screel Hill with its higher neighbour of Bengairn to make a satisfying circuit.

SCREEL HILL DERIVES from the Gaelic 'sgritheall' (scree hill) and has the accolade of being the most southerly hill in this book, being on the same latitude as Carlisle and Newcastle. Its ascent is a fairly easy undertaking on good forestry tracks and paths and begins at Screel Wood car park, just off a minor road near the A711 between Dalbeattie and Kirkcudbright.

Follow the forestry track round a couple of big bends for about 0.5km, where you will reach a junction. Straight ahead is the start of a walking trail which ascends the south-east ridge of the hill. To the left

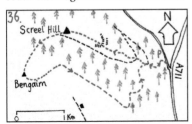

is a forest track with a gate; this is your return route. Go straight ahead and follow the walking trail upwards through the trees to meet another forest track in about 250m. The trail continues upwards from here, but may be closed due to fallen trees or forest operations. In this case, go left along the forest track, which runs parallel to the walking trail at a lower height on the south-west flank of the hill. This alternative route can be used as a return route if you want to omit the ascent of Bengairn.

Continue upwards through the forest canopy, where the path is sometimes not obvious. Recent clear-felling may also add to the uncertainty. Emerge from the trees after about 0.5km to open hillside dotted with crags and smaller outcrops. Higher up, a seat is a good excuse to stop and absorb the now extensive view of coastline and islands.

Screel Hill

From here, continue upwards on the path and take a right-hand fork which leads up on to the craggy south-east top of the hill. This is not the highest point, however, but is a better viewpoint than the true summit, 500m further west.

A vague path continues onwards through boggy hollows between crags, eventually reaching the considerable cairn marking the summit of Screel Hill.

A steep path descends the northern spur of the hill to reach a dry stone wall. If you wish to return to the start, turn left here and follow the path going below the summit which links with the forest track alternative route mentioned previously.

To continue to Bengairn, follow the dry stone wall along a clear-felled

area for a few hundred metres before ascending the slope on your left on a rough track. This goes over some minor bumps until another dry stone wall is visible below, with a wooden gate. Descend to the gate and go through it. Ascend the slope beyond through clingy heather to the grassy summit of Bengairn crowned with a trig point and several small cairns.

Ordnance Survey markings indicate that this summit held some sort of ancient fortification or burial cairn, and the amount of rocks and stone here would appear to reflect this.

Descend roughly south-east from Bengairn along the ridge, before dropping down to the left into a grassy hollow, making for the forest edge below Mid Hill, the forested hill

The summit of Screel Hill

between Bengairn and Screel Hill. Here, a fairly new forest track runs south-east, linking with an older track going back to the start.

Contour across the lower slope of Bengairn and go through a gate leading to a wide gravelly area, marking the end of the forest track.

Turn right and follow the track parallel with the Troudale Burn, before it turns and makes a few wide bends to an open grassy area where there is a fine view up to Screel Hill. Another big bend takes you to the gate near the start of the walking trail and the forest track to the car park.

37. CAIRNSMORE OF DEE (OR BLACK CRAIG OF DEE) (493M/1,617FT)

MAP	OS SHEET 77 (GR 584758)
DISTANCE	13KM
ASCENT	410M
TIME	3.5–4.5 HRS
ACCESS	DESCRIBED ROUTE: CLATTERINGSHAWS VISITOR CENTRE CAR PARK (GR 552763); FOREST DRIVE LOWER CAR PARK (GR 547752)
	DIRECT ROUTE: UPPER FOREST DRIVE CAR PARK (GR 572745)
DIFFICULTY	FOREST TRACK WITH TUSSOCKY, PATHLESS TERRAIN NEAR SUMMIT
SUMMARY	Cairnsmore of Dee is a shapely little hill in the southern part of the Galloway Forest Park. It stands proudly above Clatteringshaws Loch, with tremendous summit views to the higher Galloway Hills.

There's Cairnsmore o' Fleet
and Cairnsmore o' Dee
and Cairnsmore of Carsphairn
– the biggest of the three.

THE ANONYMOUS RHYME above refers to the three Galloway hills called Cairnsmore (from the Gaelic '*carn mor*', meaning big rocky hill) – the first, the most southerly Graham (and Donald), the second, a Marilyn (and Hugh) and the third, a Corbett (and Donald). Having been on all three, I would argue that the view from the 'wee-est of the three' easily surpasses that of the other two – often the case with smaller hills, but especially with Hughs.

It should be noted that the middle section of the described walk is wildest Galloway, off-trail, tussocky, walker-unfriendly terrain, particularly the stretch between Benniguinea (a subsidiary top) and the main summit. If you're not cursing and swearing on this section then you probably found a better route than I did!

The described route is circular, beginning and ending on good forestry tracks. If you really want to do a quick up and down, then begin at the Forest Drive upper car park, which is only 2km from the summit, the route being part of the descent

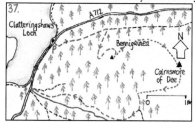

Clatteringshaws Loch from Cairnsmore of Dee

route in the circular walk.

For the described route, park at the Clatteringshaws Visitor Centre car park at Clatteringshaws Loch, on the A712 New Galloway–Newton Stewart road. Walk across the road and follow the vehicle track opposite, which eventually leads to a viewpoint of the loch. The track soon enters a forest and gains height gradually. Take a right fork after 1.5km and ignore the wee path going off to the right after several hundred metres. The track soon makes a hairpin bend and emerges from the forest, before looping round to reach the radio mast and cairn at the top of Benniguinea Hill. The view of the loch and surrounding hills from here is very fine.

The awkward middle stretch of the walk now follows, taking you to the main summit, due east of here and very obvious. Retrace your steps to the bend in the track north-east of the mast and leave the track to follow the north-east spur of Benniguinea on very rough ground. Reach the broad col, where the going is very slow, on tussocks and underlying bog. The final slopes on to Cairnsmore are marginally easier by making use of granite slabs higher up. At the summit, where there is a cairn and trig point, you can enjoy a well-earned breather and glorious views.

To descend, head due south on excellent granite slabs and outcrops until the broad ridge beings to level off at the 'Rig of Craig Gilbert'. Turn right to descend the hill's western flank heading for a firebreak and track just above the Laggan of Dee. At the time of writing, the forest had been clear-felled and the route was very obvious. Turn left along the track and reach the junction with Forest Drive, also known as the Raiders' Road – so-named because stolen cattle were once driven along here by the Black Water of Dee, as dramatised in SR Crockett's 19th-century novel *The Raiders*.

Turn right along the Raiders' Road, passing the farm at Laggan of Dee and the Upper Forestry car park. This leads within 3km to the A712, where you turn right, passing the Clatteringshaws Dam, to your starting point.

38. CRAIGLEE (ABOVE LOCH DEE) (531M/1,742FT)

MAP	OS SHEET 77 (GR 462801)
DISTANCE:	14KM
ASCENT	400M
TIME	4–6 HRS
ACCESS	GLEN TROOL UPPER CAR PARK (GR 415804)
DIFFICULTY	GOOD TRACKS INITIALLY, THEN ROUGH, PATHLESS TERRAIN
SUMMARY	Craiglee's central position in the Glentrool forest and its close proximity to several scenic lochs make it one of the finest viewpoints in Galloway. Despite being surrounded by higher hills on all sides, it has a charm and character which the hill connoisseur will find hard to resist.

THE PRESENCE OF glacial lochs, craggy hills and forest give the area of the Galloway Forest Park a rugged wilderness charm easily on a par with many Highland locations. The region has been referred to as the 'Lake District' – or should it be 'Loch District' – of southern Scotland. Comparisons are fickle, however, and the Galloway Hills have a unique quality, partly due to their underlying granite construction.

Craiglee can be approached either from the east at Craigencallie near Clatteringshaws Loch, or from the west in Glen Trool. The latter approach is shorter, more scenic and involves no monotonous forestry track walking as does the eastern option.

Park in Glen Trool at the end of the public road, where there are two parking areas within 300m of each other. This is the starting point of the

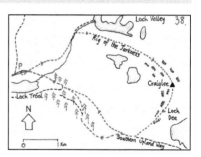

ascent of The Merrick, the highest hill in the Southern Uplands. At the end of the road, descend a gravel zigzag path on the right and follow signs for Gairland Burn and Loch Valley. After about 0.5km, a small, grassy path (signposted) branches off the main trail on the left and makes a rising traverse through bracken, of the southern flank of Buchan Hill. This path is poorly maintained and a number of large boulders will need to be negotiated higher up.

About 2km from the fork, you

The summit of Craiglee

should find yourself close to the Gairland Burn on the right with steep grassy slopes on either side. The route now leaves the path, crosses the burn and ascends the slope on the opposite side. After heavy rain, the burn may be quite swollen, but it splits into several courses in parts, making the crossing easier.

A little over 100m of ascent takes you up onto the crest of the long ridge which leads to the summit of Craiglee. This ridge is delightfully named 'Rig of the Jarkness', an almost Tolkienesque sounding name which would not be out of place in *Lord of the Rings*. 'Rig' is an Old Scots word for ridge. The derivation of Jarkness is lost in the mists of time, the loch below steep slopes to the north is Loch Valley.

The 3km ridge involves several short ascents and descents, following an intermittent path through the heather and tussocky grass. Enjoy a grand retrospective view of beautiful Loch Trool, nestling serenely between wooded slopes. About 1km from the summit, pass the tiny, idyllic Dow Loch, before reaching pockets of craggy, granite slabs and several false summits. The actual summit consists of a trig point perched on a huge granite block, from where you can really appreciate the surrounding panorama.

It is said that at least eight lochs can be seen from the summit and it is left to the reader-walker to name them all. As there are two Craiglees in Galloway, each is referred to by the name of the loch which it stands above. In this case it is Loch Dee, the conspicuous body of water south-east of the summit. Craiglee has its own two major hill lochs, the Long Loch of Glenhead and the Round Loch of Glenhead, to the west.

To return, descend by the well-defined south-west ridge, where there are some interesting, natural granite steps, making for a quick descent. Lower down, however, the going becomes very soft and tussocky, with some awkward little burns to cross. In about 2km, reach a good vehicle track, the line of the Southern Upland Way (SUW). Turn right and follow this track west.

The original line of the Southern Upland Way stays on the track as it descends to Glenhead after going through a forest plantation. However, there is also now an alternative route which branches off to the right at GR 449787 to adopt an unforested hill route, both meeting up again just west of the house at Glenhead. Forestry operations may necessitate the use of this alternative – I speak from experience!

Cross the bridge over the Glenhead Burn to reach a good vehicle track which is followed back to the car park in under 2km.

The large granite boulder, known as Bruce's Stone, is adjacent to the car park and should not be missed. The stone is a memorial to Robert the Bruce and to his victory over an English force in 1307. The battle occurred on the other side of Loch Trool, where a small band of Scots hurled boulders down the hillside, routing 2,000 English.

39. CRAIGLEE (ABOVE LOCH DOON) (523M/1,716FT)

MAP	OS SHEET 77 (GR 471963)
DISTANCE	7KM
ASCENT	340M
TIME	2.5–3.5 HRS
ACCESS	DESCRIBED CIRCULAR ROUTE: FOREST DRIVE CAR PARK (GR 477942)
	DIRECT ROUTE: LOCH DOON CASTLE CAR PARK (GR 483950)
DIFFICULTY	REASONABLE PATH BECOMING ROUGH AND INDISTINCT
SUMMARY	Like its Loch Dee namesake, Craiglee stands proudly above several scenic lochs and in particular, Loch Doon, the largest freshwater loch in southern Scotland. Craiglee is a wee gem of the Galloway Hills and a marvellous viewpoint.

TO REACH LOCH DOON and Craiglee by car, turn off the A713 just south of Dalmellington, on a minor road signposted to Loch Doon. The castle is about 9 miles along this road on the right-hand side, where there is a small parking area. The castle used to be situated on a island in the loch and was subsequently moved, stone by stone, to its present position, when the

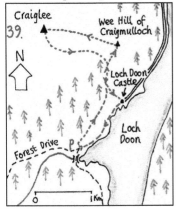

level of the loch was raised by 11m for a new hydro-electric scheme. Constructed in the 14th century, Loch Doon Castle was the maternal home of Robert the Bruce and has a rich history.

To the left of the castle, a sign saying 'Craiglea Trail' indicates the start of a path going up the hill behind the castle. If you follow the described route, this will be your return trail. Note that the spelling of Craiglee on the sign is different from the normal spelling – possibly to differentiate it from the 'Loch Dee' Craiglee.

To reach the start of the described route, continue along the road and track for 1km to reach another parking area at the start of the Forest Drive. Walking over the bridge on the track south of here gives a fine view of Loch Doon and Craiglee.

Above the track is an information board and another sign saying

Craiglee and Loch Doon

'Craiglea Trail', which marks the start of the route. The path is initially a well-made granite gravel surface, winding its way up to a viewpoint and seat. The main path to Craiglee branches off to the right before the viewpoint and deteriorates to more of a grassy runnel through heather and pockets of spruce trees.

Follow this for about 1.5km until it meets up with the main trail from the castle car park, on the lower slopes of the 'Wee Hill of Craigmulloch', the eastern outlier of Craiglee. Continue upwards, ignoring any left-hand forks, onto the summit of the Wee Hill of Craigmulloch, where the marked trail disappears near an obvious granite outcrop. The summit cairn on a small knoll just beyond is a superb viewpoint for Loch Doon, the Rhinns of Kells and the Merrick Hills.

The main summit of Craiglee lies just over 1km west of here and is reached by first descending 50m to the broad, boggy col, before the final 150m ascent of tussocky terrain and minor granite outcrops takes you to the cairn. This is not the summit, however, and the trig point lies a further 300m west.

The summit views are extensive, with lochs and hills in all directions. Loch Finlas is very prominent to the north, Loch Bradan to the west and, of course, Loch Doon to the east, while a sprinkling of smaller lochs lie to the south. Far off to the west, on a clear day, the top third of Ailsa Craig is visible.

View from the summit of Craiglee

Return to the col and avoid re-ascent by skirting round the south of the Wee Hill of Craigmulloch above the trees, to meet the ascent trail. Follow it downwards over a forest track and through an old stone sheep fank to emerge on the road by the castle. Turn right and follow the road and track for just over 1km to your starting point.

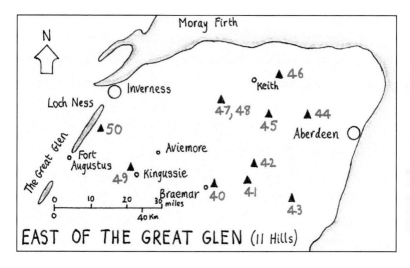

40. CREAG CHOINNICH MOSSY ROCK (538M/1,765FT)

MAP	OS SHEET 43 (GR 161918)
DISTANCE	3KM
ASCENT	220M
TIME	1–2 HRS
ACCESS	BRAEMAR (GR 150915)
DIFFICULTY	WELL-DEFINED PATH TO THE SUMMIT
SUMMARY	Braemar's own little hill of Creag Choinnich is a popular walk and an easy way to gain height and appreciate the stunning Cairngorm panorama to the north and west.

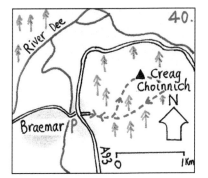

FROM THE A93 through Braemar, walk east up the minor road to the left of the church. There is a signpost saying 'Creag Choinnich and other walks'. After about 0.5km, go through a gate and turn left onto a path which is signposted to Creag Choinnich. The path winds its way up the hillside through stands of tall Scots Pines, before reaching more open heather slopes offering a fine view of Braemar.

You will soon reach the top of the

Braemar from Creag Choinnich

The Cairngorms from Creag Choinnich

hill, marked by two large summit cairns and other smaller ones dotted about on various minor spurs and knolls. The sheer number of cairns and other oddities is testament to the number of visitors this fine wee viewpoint receives – and what a viewpoint! To the north, the massive hulk of the Ben Avon massif is peppered with granite tors, while further west, the giants of Ben MacDui, Cairn Toul and Braeriach jostle for attention. The prominent hill to the south-west is Morrone (or Morven), a Corbett, and another popular ascent from Braemar.

A circular route can be accomplished by going east from the summit on a minor path, which gradually swings round to the south to reach the main path heading west back to the gate and the start.

41. THE COYLES OF MUICK (601M/1,972FT)

MAP	OS SHEET 44 (GR 329910)
DISTANCE	15KM
ASCENT	380M
TIME	4.5–5.5 HRS
ACCESS	B976 NORTH OF LOCH ULLACHIE (GR 341951)
DIFFICULTY	MIXTURE OF GOOD VEHICLE TRACKS AND PATHLESS SUMMIT TERRAIN
SUMMARY	The Coyles of Muick is an ideal introduction to more serious hillwalking in the Cairngorms. With its distinctive profile, unusual geology and massive cairn, the hill's character and charm is not in doubt.

'COYLE' (PRONOUNCED 'KEIL') possibly derives from the Gaelic 'coille', meaning wood. Rather confusingly, 'The Coyles of Muick' refers to the summit in question individually, and *also* to the group of hills between Glen Muick and Glen Girnock, including Meall Dubh and Craig of Loinmuie, which lie just to its north.

The Coyles of Muick can be ascended from any one of a number of points on the minor road west of the River Muick, using forestry tracks. However, the finest route starts near Loch Ullachie and traverses most of the ridge north of the hill, returning by the tranquil and pretty Glen Girnock to the west. This involves a river crossing, however, which may not be practicable after heavy rain.

Park on the B976 south of the River Dee, almost 2 miles west of the junction with the Glen Muick road. There is a gate to the forest track which begins just beyond Loch Ullachie and there is a small parking area across the road. Go through the gate and follow the forest track past Loch Ullachie as it climbs up to reach the edge of the forest after 1.5km. Turn left here and follow an unmade, but good path which keeps to the edge of the forest and the ridge-line of small, heathery hills. The views soon open up and the summit of The Coyles of Muick

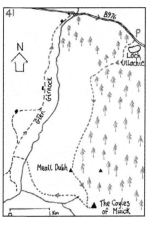

The Coyles of Muick

is very distinctive with its large cairn.

Around Meall Dubh, the path becomes less distinct and boggy as it traverses the east flank of the hill, but soon improves again on the final approach. An arc of low crags lies below the summit and the path swings right to avoid this. Oddly, the rock around here is not the usual Cairngorm granite, but a gnarled, softer rock called serpentine (magnesium silicate). The path reaches a col between two distinct little summits. To the left is a huge cairn, though now partly destroyed on its south-west side. To the right is a craggy wee summit with a small cairn, which is marginally higher and the true summit.

On a clear day it is the 'steep frowning glories of dark Lochnagar' to the south-west which really catch the eye, Lochnagar being almost twice the height of The Coyle.

To reach Glen Girnock, descend north-west into the broad depression between The Coyles of Muick and Meall Dubh. Easy slopes lead down to a burn which is followed to the Girnock Burn on tussocky grass. The glen track is visible on the opposite side of the Girnock Burn, which should be crossable on stepping-stones.

Once on the track, it is excellent walking for 5km to the road. Glen Girnock has a lonely, peaceful air with much forest regeneration on the lower reaches. At the road, turn right over the bridge and reach your starting point in under 2km.

Summit of the Coyles of Muick

42. CRAIGENDARROCH ROCKY HILL OF THE OAK WOOD (402M/1,319FT)

MAP	OS SHEET 44 (GR 365965)
DISTANCE	2KM
ASCENT	200M
TIME	1–1.5 HRS
ACCESS	BALLATER (GR 365955)
DIFFICULTY	EXCELLENT PATHS, SOME STEEP SECTIONS
SUMMARY	This popular wee hill, rising directly to the north of Ballater, on Deeside, is held dear in the hearts of local folk, not least because of its wonderful oak woods, but also its intimate charm, which is difficult to explain until you have climbed it.

SO POPULAR IS this hill, that it would be difficult not to meet someone, somewhere on its ample wooded slopes, at almost any time of day. The hill is crisscrossed with walking trails, some well constructed, others shortcuts to and from the summit.

From the centre of Ballater, walk along the A93 Braemar road and take the last street on the right, named Craigendarroch Walk. Go through the gate at the foot of the hill and turn left to follow a path which contours all the way round the hill. After about 500m, turn right onto a path which

zigzags up the hill and is marked with black arrows. Towards the top, the going is steeper but made easier by granite-block steps.

The summit area consists of a massive outcrop of ice-scoured granite with a view indicator, seat and, slightly lower, a huge cairn overlooking Ballater. Owing to the presence of trees, views in other directions are slightly restricted, but there is a feeling of being much higher than the true height.

A path continues from the summit indicator, descending in a north-

Craigendarroch from Ballater

The summit of Craigendarroch

easterly direction through pine woods before turning right and zigzagging down to the lower path, circumnavigating the hill. Emerge from the hill into a new housing estate and turn right here. This takes you back to the start of the main route in less than 1km.

43. CLACHNABEN (589M/1,932FT)

MAP	OS SHEET 45 (GR 615865)
DISTANCE	16KM
ASCENT	530M
TIME	4–5 HRS
ACCESS	GLEN DYE CAR PARK (GR 649867)
DIFFICULTY	EXCELLENT ASCENT AND DESCENT PATHS
SUMMARY	Along with Bennachie, Clachnaben is one of the most familiar and distinctive hills in north-east Scotland, purely because of its obvious granite tor near the summit (see the rhyming couplet heading Route 44). The described route is a fine, longish, circular walk.

CLACHNABEN IS KNOWN locally as Clochna'bain and the name derives from the Gaelic '*clach na beinne*' or 'stone of the hill'. The rocky wart on the hill is very prominent when driving over the high pass known as Cairn o'Mount, between Fettercairn and Banchory.

The main route to the hill begins on this road, the B974, less than 1km north of the bridge over River Dye, where there is a small parking area on the left – west of the road.

A good path leads south-west through a fine forest of Scots Pine then by a left fork downhill by the forest edge past Glendye Lodge. Cross the Mill Burn on a small bridge, before taking a right fork up a well-made track. The construction and upkeep of the paths around Clachnaben

is due to the Clachnaben Path Trust, formed in 1997.

The hill's distinctive rocky top is well seen during the ascent through attractive stands of Scots Pine and the climb is made easier by some excellent stone steps on the eastern flank of the hill. Reach the eastern face of the rocky tor and follow the path round to its right. The top of the tor can be

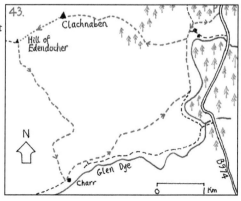

En route to Clachnaben

reached by an easy scramble on the west side and is 10m higher than the trig point, about 150m further west.

Clachnaben is held in high regard with locals and is the focus of many stories and poems. In one poem by David Grant, called 'The Muckle Spate o' Twenty-Nine', referring to

The summit tor of Clachnaben

the great floods of 1829, a character called Meg Hill, or Birlin' Meg, raced to the summit to escape the flood, where 'the angels micht rax [reach] doon for us'.

It is a good idea to make a circumnavigation of the tor – you can really gain an appreciation of its steepness and height on the eastern side.

From the trig point, follow the path south-west along the broad, heathery ridge to the Hill of Edendocher, just over 1km away. This is a grand, high-level ridge walk with fine views to Mount Battock, a Corbett.

A rough vehicle track leads downhill from here to a broad shoulder, before swinging right, then left down to the locked bothy of Charr in Glen Dye.

At Charr, turn left to follow a good vehicle track, which contours along the lower hillside above the river, past a small reservoir on the right. In about 5km of very pleasant walking, this leads back to the wee bridge over the Mill Burn. Retrace your outward route from here back to the car park to complete a very pleasing circuit.

44. BENNACHIE: MITHER TAP (518M/1,698FT)

MAP	OS SHEET 38 (GR 682224)
DISTANCE	14KM
ASCENT	540M
TIME	4–6 HRS
ACCESS	DESCRIBED ROUTE: ESSON CAR PARK, LOWER WOODEND (GR 673190) QUICKEST ROUTE: VISITOR CENTRE NEAR TULLOS (GR 698216) QUICK ROUTE, POPULAR: PITTODRIE FARM CAR PARK (GR 692244) FOR OXEN CRAIG ONLY: BACK O'BENNACHIE CAR PARK (GR 660245)
DIFFICULTY	EXCELLENT ASCENT AND DESCENT PATHS
SUMMARY	Bennachie is one of the most popular hills in north-east Scotland and Aberdeenshire's favourite. Along with Clachnaben, 35km to the south, it is topped by a prominent granite tor and is a distinctive landmark from both land and sea. Hence the couplet below.

Clachnaben and Bennachie
Are twa landmarks frae the sea.

BENNACHIE, PRONOUNCED 'bain-a-hee', is most likely derived from '*beinn chioch*' meaning hill of breasts. The name does not refer to a single hill, but to an east–west ridge with several tors and tops, the highest being Oxen Craig, pronounced 'ow-sin', (528m). However, the best known, the most prominent and the most shapely summit is called the Mither Tap, old Scots for Mother Top. She is certainly a matriarch with attitude.

Given the number of possible routes to the hill, its popularity is undeniable and it is an ideal hill for a complete traverse using two cars; the best being Back o'Bennachie to Esson,

via Millstone Hill. The finest circular route, however, begins and ends at Esson and includes the fine wee southern outlier of Millstone Hill.

Esson car park is situated about 4 miles north of the village of Monymusk on the minor road north

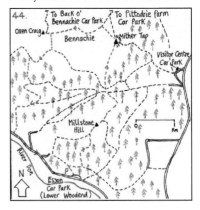

Bennachie from Millstone Hill

of the River Don. Park at Lower Woodend where there is a 'Donview' sign.

The route you are following initially is signposted 'Millstone Hill Trail' and for the first 10 minutes of walking has many left and right turns, but is well signposted. The trail gradually gains height through the pine forest, with a long series of well constructed steps, and higher up, granite-block steps. Scots Pine and silver birch dominate until you reach more open heathland, where the path soon takes you on to the summit of Millstone Hill. From here, there is a grand view of the elegant cone of Mither Tap, 2km to the north.

Descend Millstone Hill by the path heading north-east down to a plantation. Shortly after entering the forest, the path swings left in a north-westerly direction to reach a vehicle track which traverses the col between the two hills. Turn left on the track and almost immediately right onto another trail which ascends north through trees and open, heathery hillside to the summit of Mither Tap.

The granite tor at the top is a sizeable hunk of rock rising to a height of 25m in places. Its top can be reached by any number of easy scrambles, though the easiest route ascends from the east, where there are obvious remains of an Iron Age fort. A vast amount of rocks and stones was brought up the hill to erect the fort and there were at least 10 buildings and a well.

Mither Tap from Oxen Craig

The top contains a trig point and a view indicator, and is a unique vantage point for a vast tract of north-east Scotland's rolling farmland, heather moors and forests. The highest point of Oxen Craig lies 2km to the west, and although 10m higher, it pales in the shadow of Mither Tap.

To reach it, follow an obvious gravel path westward across the broad heathery col. The summit has a small granite tor and another view indicator. There is also a signpost for the Back o'Bennachie car park to the north.

Descend Oxen Craig by retracing your steps eastward for 300m before turning right on a path which descends to a path signposted 'Morton's Way Trail'. Turn right along this trail as it contours round the southern spur of Oxen Craig for about 1km. Turn left down a rough vehicle track, following the edge of a forest, to reach a forestry track where you turn right and descend through the forest in a series of zigzags to eventually reach Mill of Tilliefoure. From here, a little path goes through fields between fences to reach a house and the road by the River Don. Turn left and follow the road for about 2.5km back to the car park.

45. TAP O'NOTH (563M/1,848FT)

MAP	OS SHEET 37 (GR 484293)
DISTANCE	5KM
ASCENT	280M
TIME	1.5–2 HRS
ACCESS	HOWTON CAR PARK (GR 481284)
DIFFICULTY	WELL-DEFINED, THOUGH CIRCUITOUS PATH
SUMMARY	The distinctive truncated cone of Tap o'Noth is a prominent landmark from many parts of Aberdeenshire. A hill steeped in history and legend, its summit contains the substantial remains of the second highest vitrified hill fort in Scotland.

THE NAME 'TAP O'NOTH' derives from the Gaelic '*taip a'nochd*' (look-out top), and the hill stands north-east of the village of Rhynie. It is a popular wee hill which is easily climbed by way of a good, though rather circuitous path.

Park in the purpose-built car park just off the A941 at Howton, about 1½ miles from Rhynie. The path goes up over a stile and through a small wooded area to emerge at a vehicle track contouring round the base of the hill. Turn left along the track then right just before a gate, to follow a path uphill by the side of a forest plantation. This path ascends the hill gradually, before making a hairpin bend to curve back round to the south of the hill in a rising traverse.

Just below the summit, where the path begins to swing round to the left, you can drop down to an example of what the locals call 'ferlies': large stones with historic significance, often

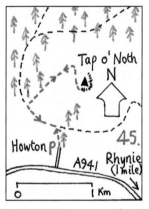

Pictish. This huge spur of rock in known as Clochmaloo after the Celtic missionary, St Moluac ('*clach*' is Gaelic for 'stone').

Back on the path, the summit is soon reached, crowned by the vitrified ruins of an Iron Age fort. The circular wall of masonry is very evident and was strengthened considerably by the act of heating and fusing (vitrifying) the rocks. Not surprisingly, this is a

Tap o'Noth

grand viewpoint, with the Buck of Cabrach very prominent to the south-west. On a clear day, you are sure to spot Ben Rinnes, Mount Keen and Lochnagar.

At one time there was a wooden hut on the summit, where a watchman looked out for fires in Clashindarroch forest to the north. It eventually fell foul of the wild weather and was demolished.

It is best to descend by the route of ascent.

46. KNOCK HILL (430M/1,412FT)

MAP	OS SHEET 29 (GR 537552)
DISTANCE	2KM
ASCENT	230M
TIME	1 HR
ACCESS	SMALL PARKING AREA (GR 547554)
DIFFICULTY	STEEP, HEATHERY PATH DIRECT TO SUMMIT
SUMMARY	The distinctive heather dome of Knock Hill is a prominent Banffshire landmark and a popular viewpoint.

THE SCOTS WORD 'knock', from the Gaelic '*cnoc*', for a conspicuous and often isolated knoll, is a perfect description of this lofty eminence, the highest point for about 22 km in all directions. Knock Hill commands a grand summit panorama and should be climbed on a clear day when the

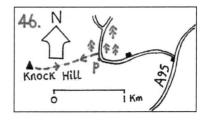

Knock Hill

view can be appreciated.

The high, heathery cone of Knock Hill looks almost out of place in the rolling farm land of Banff and Buchan. The only path to the top starts from the east at a small parking area on a minor road off the A95 Keith to Banff road. This minor road is easy to miss, but its junction with the A95 is just next to a house. Drive along the road for about 1km; past Swilebog, it makes a sharp turn to the right, where there is a parking area on the left, by a wood.

Walk along the road for about 10m and turn left through a gate to follow a path through the wood and out into open, heather-clad hillside. The path takes an uncompromising line directly up the steep slope and reaches the top in 1km.

The summit has a trig point and a memorial cairn, and gives a rare bird's-eye view of the surrounding farmland and of the Moray coast.

Although the map indicates a path traversing round the southern base of the hill, the section north of Knock Wood is now overrun by fields, ditches and fences and from experience is not walker-friendly. What would appear to be a possible circular route is therefore not practicable and the only viable return is by the ascent route.

47. MEIKLE CONVAL (571M/1,873FT)
48. LITTLE CONVAL (552M/1,811FT)

MAP	OS SHEET 28 (GR 291372, 294393)
DISTANCE	8KM
ASCENT	420M
TIME	2.5–3.5 HRS
ACCESS	BEN RINNES CAR PARK (GR 285359)
DIFFICULTY	A MIXTURE OF HEATHERY PATHS AND STONY TRACKS
SUMMARY	These two hills may not possess the allure and popularity of their higher Corbett neighbour, but they are a perfect way to escape the crowds and appreciate the spacious summit views.

SOME WOULD SAY that this pair of hills are mere outliers of Ben Rinnes and indeed the name Conval is derived from the Celtic prefix '*con*' meaning 'together' or 'with', and 'val' from '*mheall*', meaning 'hill'. Meikle means large. However, to dismiss them on this account is a great disservice as they are distinctive enough to provide a pleasant few hours of easy hillwalking. Given suitable transport arrangements, it would be a fine expedition to make a complete traverse of all three hills, using suitable paths and forest tracks.

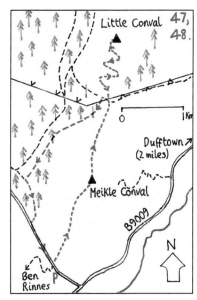

The described route begins at the Ben Rinnes starting point, at the col between this hill and the Convals. The minor road through here is signposted Edinvillie from the main B9009 Tomintoul to Dufftown road.

Directly opposite the Ben Rinnes path, a narrow path ascends through the deep heather of Meikle Conval's south-west ridge, steeply at first,

before levelling off at a broad shoulder. Another small rise lead to the summit cairn, where there is an excellent view of Ben Rinnes and of Little Conval.

Little Conval from Meikle Conval

Continue north from the summit, following a peaty path which descends to the wide col below Little Conval, going under a line of pylons. Another track ascends from the right. Cross this and follow a track zigzagging up the southern flank of Little Conval. Both this track and the one up Meikle Conval are unmarked on the current os map. Reach the summit cairn at 552m and the slightly lower trig point a short distance further on.

Descend Little Conval by the ascent route back to the col, before turning right to meet a forest track which contours round the north-western flank of Meikle Conval. This is the upper of two parallel tracks. At a track junction, 2km further on, turn left and follow another track to the edge of a plantation on the right. Turn right here and reach the road in a few hundred metres. Turn left along the road to reach the starting point in about 0.5km.

49. CREAG BHEAG LITTLE ROCK OR LITTLE CRAG (487M/1,598FT)

MAP	OS SHEET 35 (GR 745017)
DISTANCE	5 KM
ASCENT	200M
TIME	2–3 HRS
ACCESS	ARDVONIE CAR PARK IN KINGUSSIE
DIFFICULTY	MAINLY WELL-DEFINED PATHS AND TRACKS
SUMMARY	Creag Bheag stands in a strategic position in Strathspey overlooking Kingussie, with the sprawling mass of the Cairngorms to the south and the Monadhliath to the north. It is a superb little hill with a summit which is a trial to leave as the views are astounding.

THE MINI-MOUNTAIN of Creag Bheag is well seen from the A9 on the approach to Kingussie. The Ardvonie car park is on Gynack Road, which starts adjacent to the Duke of Gordon Hotel in the town centre.

Follow a sign for Creag Bheag taking you to the top corner of the park and on to a road. Turn right here and ignore the signs pointing left down West Terrace. Continue uphill until the road bends right and follow a track on the left, going through a metal gate. Walk through delightful birch then pine as the path climbs up to a gate on

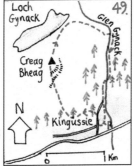

Creag Bheag from Loch Gynack

the forest edge. There is an excellent view from here of the craggy ramparts of the hill and an easy to follow trail by a dry stone wall goes all the way to the summit.

There is a confusing line of cairns along the summit ridge and it is left to the reader to decide which one is the actual top. Take time to enjoy the bird's-eye view of Kingussie ('head of the pinewood') and the distant Cairngorms, perhaps while sitting on the well-constructed stone shelter seat a short distance down the north-west ridge.

A satisfying circular walk can be made

The Cairngorms from Creag Bheag

by continuing down the north-west ridge on a steepish path to tranquil Loch Gynack, nestling between Creag Bheag and Creag Mhor. The path goes through a gate into a woodland and through another gate before passing a golf course. Cross the Gynack Burn by a wooden bridge and follow the track to reach Ardbroilach Road, where you turn right. The second signed path on the right takes you to a viewing platform above the Gynack Burn.

Robert Louis Stevenson spent much time in Kingussie in the 1880s and enjoyed long stravaigs by his 'golden burn'. Further along the path cross the Gynack by a bridge and stay on the path opposite as it descends, veering left to the car park entrance and the starting point.

Stone seat on Creag Bheag

50. STAC GORM BLUE STACK (430M/1,411FT)

MAP	OS SHEET 35 (GR 630273)
DISTANCE	2KM
ASCENT	220M
TIME	1–1.5 HRS
ACCESS	LOCH RUTHVEN NATURE RESERVE CAR PARK (GR 637281)
DIFFICULTY	ILL-DEFINED HEATHERY PATH WITH SOME ROCKY OUTCROPS
SUMMARY	This is the finest of a cluster of craggy peaklets lying to the north-east of Loch Ness. It offers a delightful short outing with superb views.

LOCH RUTHVEN NATURE RESERVE car park can be reached by leaving the A9 5 miles south of Inverness and driving along the B851 signposted to Fort Augustus. About 7 miles along this road, turn right to reach Loch Ruthven in a mile. Park in the small car park at the eastern end of the loch, which is owned by the RSPB.

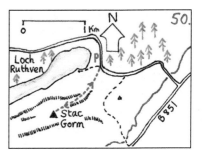

Loch Ruthven is a beautiful, peaceful stretch of water, nestling in the hills with the rocky slopes of Stac Gorm rising up directly to the south. The loch is home to half the UK population of the rare and colourful Slavonian grebe and you can read more about this on the information board.

Stac Gorm and Loch Ruthven

Loch Ruthven from Stac Gorm

On first impressions it would seem like a good outing to climb the hill by its east ridge and continue eastwards before descending north to the loch, followed by a return along the south shore. This is not recommended as there are many nesting birds along this shore and a path only goes as far as a bird hide a few hundred metres from the car park.

The described route, therefore, is an ascent and descent by the east ridge. After crossing the fence, follow a faint path heading directly towards Stac Gorm. A huge, house-sized boulder on the lower slopes of the hill is a good point to aim for if the path is too indistinct.

Beyond the boulder, the path continues upward through deep heather, before weaving its way round a series of minor crags, eventually reaching a level platform. Several more short, steep sections bring you to the narrow summit ridge and the trig point, perched on a rocky outcrop.

The views in all directions are magnificent and give a fine appreciation of the wild and neglected hinterland only a few kilometres from the northern end of Loch Ness. The view to the western end of Loch Ruthven is particularly fine.

Return by the route of ascent.

PART 2

WEST AND NORTH SCOTLAND – 50 HUGHS

THE FIRTH OF CLYDE TO FORT WILLIAM – 13 HUGHS
FORT WILLIAM TO ULLAPOOL – 15 HUGHS
THE FAR NORTH – 22 HUGHS

Maiden Pap

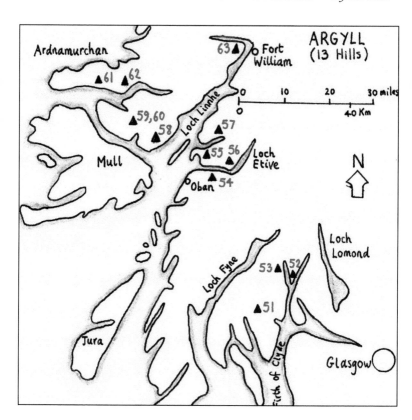

51. SGORACH MOR BIG PRONGED HILL (601M/1,972FT)

MAP	OS SHEET 56 (GR 097850)
DISTANCE	11KM
ASCENT	700M
TIME	3.5–5 HRS
ACCESS	STRATH EACHAIG (GR 139846)
DIFFICULTY	FOREST TRACKS, BUSH-WHACKING AND PATHLESS ROUGH TERRAIN
SUMMARY	Sgorach Mor, along with its neighbour, An Creachan, are two very distinctive hills forming a horseshoe above Glen Massan, near the south end of Loch Eck. The circuit of this horseshoe makes a fine expedition with exceptional views.

PARK IN STRATH EACHAIG, about 6 miles north of Dunoon, opposite a forest track. There is a sign which says 'Glen Massan – no access for vehicles'. Walk up this track and take the left fork after 1km, just before an open field and a white house, 'Corarsik', which takes the name of the forested glen which you will be walking through. The track winds its way upwards on the south side of the Corarsik Burn for about 2.5km, where it suddenly appears to end at a boggy, grassy area.

From here, route-finding can be quite tricky, but a small path continues upwards on the right, with logs crossing the boggier sections. Reach an old wooden hide, where you turn left to climb up through the trees (some bush-whacking required!) for several hundred metres, to reach open hillside

below Sgorach Mor.

Ascend easy, grassy slopes to 'Point 579' and the summit ridge leading to the final craggy knoll, on top of which there is a small cairn. There is a fine view down to Loch Tarsan, which is dammed in two places, and Loch Striven is just visible beyond. Cruach Neuran is very prominent to the south, where the Graham of Cruach nan Capull can also be seen.

Descend north-west to the wide col, before turning east to climb the fine, craggy promontory of An Creachan (meaning, literally, 'bare summit of a

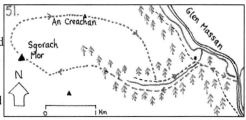

Summit cone of Sgorach Mor

hill') and the finest viewpoint of the round. From the trig point, there is a grand view south-east to Holy Loch, Dunoon, and across the Firth of Clyde to Greenock.

Descend south-east, staying on the ridge, to traverse a minor top, before following a minor spur downwards to the forest edge. A small stream marks the start of a firebreak which takes you down in 400m to an old forestry track, where you turn left. This track is very boggy in places and has deteriorated through lack of use and upkeep. In less than 1km reach the white house ('Corarsik') and turn right to reach the track back to the starting point.

Sgorach Mor summit

52. CLACH BHEINN STONE HILL (441M/1,447FT)

MAP	OS SHEET 56 (GR 211954)
DISTANCE	16KM
ASCENT	470M
TIME	5–7 HRS
ACCESS	LOCHGOILHEAD (GR 200013)
DIFFICULTY	GOOD TRACKS AND PATHLESS ROUGH CENTRAL SECTION
SUMMARY	Clach Bheinn occupies a stunning position at the end of the Ardgoil peninsula, an area dominated by long sea lochs and rugged mountains. The summit panorama is spectacular.

LYING BETWEEN LOCH LONG and Loch Goil, the Ardgoil peninsula contains a spine of craggy mountains, from the Graham of Cnoc Coinnich in the north to wee Clach Bheinn in the south. Of the four peaks in the chain, Clach Bheinn may be the lowest, but is without a doubt the finest viewpoint and the craggiest. The traverse of all four summits along the knobbly backbone of the peninsula would be a splendid expedition, but the described route ascends Clach Bheinn only, by a largely circular tour.

Park in the Lochgoilhead car park at the head of Loch Goil. Do not attempt to drive further south along the lochside as there are

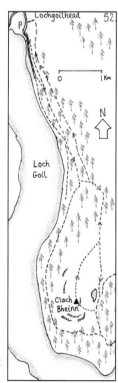

no viable parking spaces; signs direct you to park in the village.

Walk south along the narrow road on the east side of Loch Goil past several houses until a path appears on the left, ascending the wooded slope. This is marked by a signpost and is over 1km from the start. Follow the path upwards to a forestry track and walk southwards along it for about 2km until you reach a second path junction on the left with a signpost.

Take this path as it climbs steeply upwards through pleasant, broadleaf forest for a few hundred metres, before reaching a more substantial path which contours along the

Loch Goil from Clach Bheinn

hillside. The left branch of this path is not marked on older maps as it is a relatively recent cycle/walking route going back to Lochgoilhead. It forms the last part of this route description and is known locally as the Duke's Pass, a route following an old drovers' path from Lochgoilhead to a ferry crossing of Loch Long. The Duke in question was the Duke of Argyll, who owned the whole area.

Turn along the right branch of the Duke's Pass, as it gradually ascends the forested hillside, crossing some streams higher up.

After about 1.5km, you will emerge from an area of new Sitka Spruce forest with a fine view south to Corran Lochan, nestling below the steep slopes of Clach Bheinn,

now visible on the right. 'Corran' is Gaelic for 'tapering point of land'. The walk to Corran Lochan from the forest edge is beautifully secluded and the little lochan itself is idyllic and very peaceful. The area around the lochan was known in cattle-droving days as '*buaile a'ghrianain*', meaning 'cattlefold of the sunny hillock', the hillock being Clach Bheinn. The name became anglicised into 'bowling green' and the name 'Argyll's Bowling Green' appears on early maps of the area.

The path meets a forestry track on the east side of the lochan, where there is a picnic table, an odd sight in such a remote location. Turn right along the forest track for about 400m, where the craggy eastern spur of the hill can be gained at the point where the forest edge lies very close to the track. Climb the hillside, which is dotted with rhododendrons and gradually turn round to the right, up a grassy hollow, to reach the summit area of the hill.

The trig point stands on one of several little rocky knolls but this is not the highest point, which is a short distance to the north on another knoll – a glorious spot to sit and stare at the cracking views in all directions, especially south, down Loch Long and Gare Loch, and north up Loch Goil to the Arrochar Alps skyline.

Continue northwards over several humps and hollows to gain an excellent view along the blue expanse of Loch Goil to Lochgoilhead. The knobbly ridge can be followed as far as you please, before descending to the right to regain the path of approach.

Follow the path through the forest and continue along its northern extension, which runs parallel to the forestry track lower down. This path goes all the way to Lochgoilhead where it meets the long-distance Cowal Way just above the village. Follow this down to the village and your starting point.

53. CRUACH NAM MISEAG HEAP OR STACK OF THE KID (606M/1,988FT)

MAP	OS SHEET 56 (GR 183981)
DISTANCE	7KM
ASCENT	600M
TIME	3–4 HRS
ACCESS	LETTERMAY (GR 188003)
DIFFICULTY	MAINLY ROUGH, COMPLEX, PATHLESS TERRAIN
SUMMARY	This is a fine, topographically complex little hill, rising steeply from the western shore of Upper Loch Goil. Its unique character sets it apart from its Corbett neighbour of Beinn Bheula to the west.

MANY PEOPLE WILL consider climbing both Beinn Bheula and Cruach nam Miseag together in a single, high-level circuit and this would be a superb expedition. However, the described route is the ascent of 'Cruach' only. The hill is almost totally surrounded by commercial forestry and a path along the western flank of the hill, following the line of a firebreak, has been almost totally

decimated by recent clearfelling – it wasn't that great even prior to this! The described route makes use of a recently constructed walkers' path up the north side of the hill, which ascends to just beyond the tree-line – a godsend. The only worthy circular route is to include Beinn Bheula.

On the drive down the B839 road from the 'Rest and Be Thankful' pass, take the minor road right (just before Lochgoilhead) signposted 'Carrick Castle'. Park at a small lay-by immediately before the turn-off track on the right to Lettermay.

Walk up the track past Lettermay House and go left behind some newer houses. Just ahead, the track makes a big turn to the right near the entrance to another recently built house and heads west into the forest, gradually ascending. Just after another bend to the left about 1km further on, you should spot the start of a path on the left, heading upwards through the forest.

Follow this path, steeply at first,

Cruach nam Miseag from Ben Bheula

as it climbs through the dense mass of Sitka Spruce. The path is well-constructed and, at the time of writing, fallen trees had been cleared from it. Reach the forest edge, where the path continues to ascend and makes a sharp bend to the left. Soon after this point, the path degenerates into a grassy furrow by a ditch and it is best to break away and make a direct ascent of the open hillside.

The ascent is characterised by long grassy ramps and assorted rocky outcrops. The view northwards to the sheltered little hamlet of Lochgoilhead with its scattered houses and yachts on the loch, is very picturesque.

As you gain height, you begin to appreciate the interesting topography of the hill. The summit area is a cluster of craggy knolls and in mist would be very tricky to navigate. The actual summit cairn is tiny; perched on the grassy top of the highest knoll, it is a superb viewpoint, especially southwards along Loch Goil to Loch Long.

On a recent ascent of this hill I dropped down westwards to Lochain nan Cnaimh and returned by the 'path' mentioned earlier. Clear-felling on the west side of the hill has rendered this route as good as useless and it is not recommended.

The best option is to return by the route of ascent, remembering to stay left above the tree-line to rendezvous with the forest path.

54. DEADH CHOIMHEAD WATCH OR LOOK-OUT HILL (383M/1,257FT)

MAP	OS SHEET 49 (GR 947287)
DISTANCE	3KM
ASCENT	300M
TIME	1.5–2.5 HRS
ACCESS	GLEN LONAN ROAD (GR 946274)
DIFFICULTY	INTERMITTENT GRASSY PATH
SUMMARY	Deadh Choimhead is a hidden gem of a hill; craggy, prominent and a wonderful viewpoint, but so off the beaten track that it receives few visitors. Save this for a fine day, as the summit panorama is truly magnificent.

PRONOUNCED 'DIU COYUD', the name 'look-out hill' is very apt for a hill commanding superlative views. Tucked away in the green, rolling hill country east of Oban and south of Loch Etive, it is not the highest hill in the area – that accolade going to Beinn Ghlas, just 3km to the south, on the southern side of Glen Lonan.

The hill is surrounded by commercial forestry and has no apparent path to the summit, but there is access from Glen Lonan to the south on an unmarked path with a small river crossing.

Find a suitable parking spot just west of Clachadubh house, immediately south of the hill. Follow a grassy track to the river and cross it by stepping-stones or by removing boots. In spate

conditions, you may prefer to drive further west and park on the opposite side of a bridge, before following the forest edge for 1km to reach the same point. Go through a gate on the forest edge and take the path leading up to a recent forestry track which contours round the base of the hill. You will probably have to climb or go round fallen trees lying across the path.

Cross the forest track and continue upwards on the same path until you reach the top edge of the forest, just below some crags and scree. Here, a faint path makes a rising traverse off to the left, below the crags, before turning right again to reach a level area. Follow this to a higher area dotted with self-seeded Sitka Spruce and climb an easy, grassy runnel to

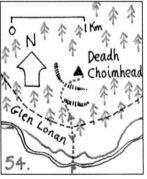

Deadh Choimhead

the right of some obvious crags.

Those wishing a more sporting ascent may consider some scrambling on these basalt crags. A final short pull leads to the small summit area, crowned with a wee cairn made from the remains of what used to be the trig point. On a clear day, the view from here rivals that of Beinn Lora to the north. The Ben Cruachan range is particularly notable to the east. Mull is very prominent to the west. This would be a fine summit to linger on during a long summer's evening, with the sun gradually dipping behind Mull. It is best to return by the route of ascent.

On the summit of Deadh Choimhead

55. BEINN LORA (308M/1,010FT)

MAP	OS SHEET 49 (GR 919377)
DISTANCE	5KM
ASCENT	300M
TIME	1.5–2.5 HRS
ACCESS	FORESTRY COMMISSION CAR PARK, BENDERLOCH (GR 905381)
DIFFICULTY	GOOD FOREST TRACKS AND WELL-MADE PATHS
SUMMARY	Beinn Lora's prime coastal position, opposite the islands of Lismore and Mull, makes for an unparalleled viewpoint in the Southern Highlands. It is a deservedly popular wee hill, largely accessible by excellent forest trails.

DESPITE ITS MODEST height, barely reaching the 1,000ft mark, Beinn Lora is a cracker of a hill, with summit views to die for, especially if you are lucky enough to watch the sun set behind the hills of Mull.

Park in the Forestry Commission car park in Benderloch, next to the petrol station, just off the A828 Oban to Fort William road. There is an information board and a sign indicating the path to Beinn Lora. At the time of writing this was marked as the blue route. Recently, there has been significant path improvement and clear-

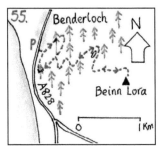

felling, with a new vehicle track higher up, and you are advised to heed any signs indicating a change of route.

Almost immediately, the trail reaches a junction and either way suffices. The described route takes the left route and returns by the right. The left trail contours along the base of the steep, wooded slope, by the backs of several houses, before ascending steeply and looping back. Massive beech trees give way to pine and spruce and the view across Ardmucknish Bay begins to open out.

The trail soon begins to ascend steeply again in a series of zigzags, with picnic tables placed at various suitable viewpoints. Shortly, you will reach a sign indicating the path to a viewpoint called the 'Eagles' Eyrie', a five-minute diversion worth the extra effort. A short section of vehicle track leads to the walking trail, which loops round a green and fertile hollow containing the reed-choked Lochan

Beinn Lora

nan Ron, where you may spot roe deer. This is followed by a short steeper section going up to the edge of the forest, where there is a gate and picnic table. The trig point on the summit of Beinn Lora is visible, less than 1km away.

The path from here to the summit is fairly obvious, but is unmade and contains some boggy sections, with duckboards in places.

The summit trig point, on a prominent little knoll, is a truly magnificent viewpoint, especially to the west, where the long island of Lismore ('big garden') is backed by the shapely Morvern hills, with the Mull mountains further south. Ben Cruachan – Argyll's highest Munro – dominates the view to the east.

Retrace your steps back to the junction with the southerly loop and turn off left here to follow the alternative route back to the car park.

Summit of Beinn Lora

56. BEINN DUIRINNIS (555M/1,821FT)

MAP	OS SHEET 50 (GR 021348)
DISTANCE	7KM
ASCENT	560M
TIME	3–5 HRS
ACCESS	BONAWE PARKING AREA (GR 012333)
DIFFICULTY	MAINLY ROUGH, CRAGGY PATHLESS TERRAIN, STEEP DESCENT
SUMMARY	A marvellously situated, craggy hill of immense character with stunning views along the length of Loch Etive.

THE ORIGIN OF Duirinnis is unclear but 'innis' refers to a green spot or pasture and 'duirc' is an acorn ('doire' is an oak copse). The lower south-eastern slopes of the hill above Loch Etive are a beautiful, green canopy of mature oak trees, so the connection seems fairly sound.

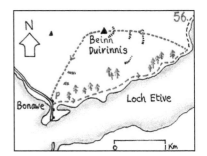

Beinn Duirinnis occupies a strategic position just north of the Loch Etive narrows and as such it offers a fine

Beinn Duirinnis

Loch Etive from Beinn Duirinnis

view of the loch and of the graceful ridges of the Ben Cruachan massif, directly across the loch. Although the hill could be dismissed as merely a minor outlier of Beinn Mheadhonach (a Graham) to the north, the summit views are arguably superior and the hill has a character and individuality deserving of Hugh status.

The ferry across the Loch Etive narrows from Taynuilt to Bonawe has long since ceased to function and if approaching the hill from the A85 you will have to cross the Connel Bridge and turn right onto the minor coastal road (B845) to reach Bonawe. Park on the large area just before the entrance to Bonawe Quarry.

Follow the sign indicating the footpath to Loch Etive. The walkers' path takes a route left of the main quarry and crosses the quarry track further on. You will have walked for over 1km before the noise of quarry machinery gradually subsides. Several signs to the left of the track instruct you not to leave the track at these points.

The peace and sylvan beauty of the area should soon assert themselves as you pass under massive mature oak trees and catch glimpses of the loch. After 3km, reach the foot of the craggy eastern spur of the hill. This provides the route of ascent.

Gain the lower grassy slopes by some unavoidable bracken-bashing, the reward being a grand view up the length of Loch Etive to the Glen Etive Munros. Interest is maintained by a

Summit of Beinn Duirinnis

prominent granite outcrop further on and several other smaller crags and fissures.

Higher up, several of these fissures provide interest and frustration in equal measure and a number of false tops appear before the true summit reveals itself as a final, steep, rocky knoll, surmounted by a sizeable cairn perched on the edge of a granite slab. At the time of writing, a rather weather-beaten Saltire fluttered its ragged remnants from the top of a metal pole.

As already remarked upon, the summit panorama is magnificent and it is hard to leave such a stunning vantage point.

Descent south-west over slabs and minor hummocks towards a flat, tussocky depression. Another small rise with a cairn soon leads to unrelenting, steep slopes which lead directly down to the road at Bonawe, several hundred metres west of the starting point. Be prepared for a tangle of bracken and trees in the lower reaches and also a few minor crags.

57. BEINN CHURALAIN (549M/ 1,800FT)

MAP	OS SHEET 49 (GR 990461)
DISTANCE	6KM
ASCENT	550M
TIME	3–4 HRS
ACCESS	CREAGAN INN CAR PARK (GR 974446)
DIFFICULTY	MAINLY GENTLE, GRASSY THOUGH PATHLESS GROUND
SUMMARY	Beinn Churalain occupies a commanding and strategic position, high above the head of Loch Creran. Like Beinn Lora, down the road, its grand coastal position make it a superlative viewpoint, with the added bonus of a welcoming pint in the Creagan Inn on your return.

BEINN CHURALAIN DOMINATES the view on the drive north from Benderloch by the shores of Loch Creran, and its long and easy south-west ridge rising from the Creagan Inn, provides the obvious route of ascent.

Park in the ample parking area outside the Inn and promise yourself a pint later! Walk north along the A828 for a few hundred metres before crossing the road to go through a gate and under a bridge arch supporting the old Oban to Ballachulish railway, long since gone. Follow a track round the back of a deserted farm building and go through a second gate near a field. Cross the small stream on your right and ascend the slope opposite by an obvious craggy spur. This leads to an area of open hillside with a sprinkling of stunted birch trees, part of the Glasdrum National Nature Reserve.

Ascend easy, grassy slopes to a gate in a dry stone. Go through the gate and continue to climb upwards, beyond the last vestiges of trees, to open hillside dotted with minor rock outcrops. As you gain height the views start to impress and are a good excuse to stop and recharge. As you are climbing from sea-level, every inch of the ascent is felt, followed by relief as the angle gradually decreases.

The first minor top with a small cairn is not the summit. At this point,

Beinn Churalain

a larger cairn on a prominent knoll beyond should be visible about 700m further on. Climb up to this cairn on an initially well-defined little spur, followed by several hummocks. The actual summit is still 200m to the north-east and is 3m higher than this cairn which is marked as 546m on the Landranger map. The large cairn is a better viewpoint however, and what a view!

Loch Creran and surrounding land dominate the view to the south-west and further west the 13th-century MacDougall stronghold of Castle Stalker is visible in Loch Laich, notable for its appearance at the end of the comedy epic *Monty Python and the Holy Grail*!

To vary the descent, drop down fairly steep, grassy slopes north-west of the summit and ascend slightly to the top of a subsidiary ridge that runs parallel with the ascent ridge. This can then be followed downwards over several minor spurs, with a fine view of the craggy north-western face of Beinn Churalain.

Lower down, enter an area of dwarf birch trees and follow the line of a fence, crossing another one en route. Below an area of bracken, go through a wooden gate and follow a stream down to the line of the old railway, and a chalet park. Turn left and walk along the line of the railway on a tarmac lane and track, past the old station building.

The railway, which opened up Oban and the west coast to tourists

Summit of Beinn Churalain

in the late 19th century, sadly closed in 1966, thanks to Dr Beeching, but the Connel Bridge to the south is still used by cars. When it was constructed, it was second in size only to the Forth Rail Bridge.

Stay on the line of the railway until the track forks off to the right, taking you onto the road and wide cycling pavement leading back to the Creagan Inn and that well deserved pint.

58. AN SLEAGHACH SPEAR-LIKE HILL (513M/1,684FT)

MAP	OS SHEET 49 (GR 764434)
DISTANCE	18KM
ASCENT	520M
TIME	5–7 HRS
ACCESS	ARDTORNISH ESTATE OFFICE (GR 705474)
DIFFICULTY	EASY VEHICLE TRACK APPROACH FOLLOWED BY PATHLESS SECTION
SUMMARY	This lonely hill gains star-quality for its position and remoteness in the southern extremity of Morvern – not a hill for the casual pedestrian.

AN SLEAGHACH WOULD certainly not feature on a list of the most popular hills in Scotland, but its remoteness and status as a superlative viewpoint give it a unique charm which will be hard to resist for lovers of Scotland's wild corners.

Access is now much easier due to a recently constructed vehicle track to Loch Tearnait, supporting a new Hydro Scheme and its extension south of the loch to within striking distance of the hill. It is now possible to cycle to within 2km of the hill's summit.

To reach the starting point, take the Ardtornish turn-off from the A884 Lochaline road, about 3 miles north of the Mull Ferry. Drive over the bridge and round the head of Loch Aline, turning left after crossing a second bridge. Park after several hundred yards on the left, at a square, near the Ardtornish Estate Office and Information Centre.

Walk up the track past several farm buildings and turn left over the bridge before turning right up a hill past two cottages. Go through a metal gate by a smaller walkers' gate on the left – the main gate is for vehicles and can only be opened electronically.

Continue uphill and round a sharp left turn to reach a recently created reservoir and dam. The track goes round the northern side of the reservoir and

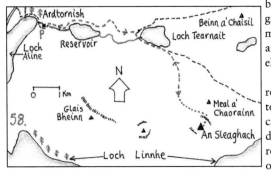

Loch Tearnait

in 2km you will reach a secondary track going off to the right to a hydro building. Ignore this and continue on the main track until you reach the attractive, natural expanse of Loch Tearnait, popular with fishermen. There is a fine MBA bothy (Leacraithnaich) just above the loch and a crannog with a lone tree in the centre of the loch. This is an ideal spot for a short rest and to absorb the peace and tranquillity.

The track winds along the southern edge of the loch and is mapped as continuing south-eastwards to the lonely settlement of Eignaig on the coast, over 5km from the loch. However, a new track now leaves the loch at GR 748467 and heads almost directly to An Sleaghach, ending at the Allt Dubh Dhoire Thearnait, which can be followed upwards by deer tracks to Lagan a'Bhuic, the wide, grassy bealach between An Sleaghach and Meal a'Chaorainn, the main hill's northerly outlier.

The final push to the summit from here is quite steep and can be enlivened by a fine scramble on some granite outcrops forming a long rib with plenty of hand-holds. The actual summit is poised airily on a prominent grassy tor littered with granite slabs and crags.

On a clear day, the view from this grand coastal hill must be superb – I was unlucky enough to be immersed in a summer heat-haze, with the distant hills faded to amorphous, monochrome shapes. Situated on

Summit of An Sleaghach

Loch Linnhe's north side, the hill has a bird's-eye view of the long, low-lying Isle of Lismore, with Mull's mountainous skyline rising up beyond the Sound of Mull. The mainland giants of Ben Cruachan, Ben Starav and Bidean Nam Bian would all be visible, but not on my visit.

Return by the ascent route, or for those with energy and inclination, a big circular route can be accomplished by traversing Mam a' Chullaich and Glas Bheinn's long north-western shoulder.

59. BEINN IADAIN HILL OF PAIN OR IVY (571M/1,873FT)
60. BEINN NA H-UAMHA HILL OF THE CAVE (465M/1,525FT)

MAP	OS SHEET 49 (GR 691561, 682534)
DISTANCE	13KM
ASCENT:	800M
TIME	5–7 HRS
ACCESS	PUBLIC ROAD END (GR 656541)
DIFFICULTY	GOOD APPROACH TRACK FOLLOWED BY WILD, PATHLESS TERRAIN
SUMMARY	This pair of hills are two craggy summits full of character tucked away in Morvern, a beautifully wild and remote region of Scotland, north of the Sound of Mull.

UNLESS YOU ARE travelling to or from Mull by the small Lochaline Ferry, the region of Morvern is likely to be off the radar of most tourists and hillwalkers. Of the half-dozen or so main hills in the area, these two are by far the most outstanding, in terms of character and attitude.

Park at the end of the public road to Rahoy, which leaves the A884 3 miles north of Lochaline. There is a parking area for around three cars.

Walk along the private road towards Rahoy, crossing River

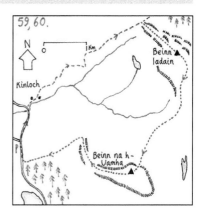

Beinn Iadain

Kinloch by a bridge, before taking the right fork towards Kinloch. Note that there may be a closed gate at the fork with what appeared to me to be a permanent stag shooting sign. If stag shooting is not in progress, or if it is a Sunday, then you have every right to walk here.

Ignoring a right fork going to Kinloch House, continue along the track as it meanders uphill through

View from Beinn na h-Uamha

pockets of oak, birch and alder. The area you are walking in, including both hills, is noted for several species of unusual flora, and is protected by 'The Rahoy Hills Wildlife Reserve'.

As you gain height, the rocky north-western ridge of Beinn Iadain becomes visible, its terraced layers of basalt very distinctive. Both hills possess the typical basaltic features of steep, terraced slopes and flat tops that are also very evident on many of Mull's smaller hills.

The track continues up Coire an Tuim beyond the point shown on the map, to the foot of the north-west ridge, at a small quarry by a knoll. Leave the track and head for the ridge, crossing a deer fence by a stile. Climb the ridge by an indistinct path on somewhat loose terrain as it weaves its way round rocky outcrops. Some easy scrambling is available for the more adventurous.

Reach the flat summit and trig point after climbing a low fence. Just beyond is a tiny lochan surrounded by small crags, an ideal lunch stop. Chances are, you will have the summit to yourself, so enjoy the views and peace.

To continue the traverse over Beinn na h-Uamha, head west of south to follow the line of the top of the crags forming the south-western escarpment of the hill. Lower down, there are a series of craggy terraces and you may need to head further east to find a suitable way down. Once below the main crags, descend south-west

Beinn na h-Uamha

on easy grass slopes to the wide col below Beinn na h-Uamha.

Ascend the hill's wide north ridge by the easiest line, avoiding any outcrops. The obvious line of crags guarding the summit plateau can be avoided by any one of several grassy ramps or gullies. The summit has a fairly large cairn and gives fine views down Loch Teacuis to the north-west.

The finest feature of the hill is its long northern bastion of basalt cliffs, the top of which can be followed on the gradual descent west. You may spot herds of deer on the grassy slopes below the cliffs. Continue following the cliff edge for 1km before reaching a flatter, grassy spur with crags on its western flank. At the end of the spur, descend west, bypassing the crags, to reach a flat area. Continue west down steeper slopes by the edge of a forest plantation to reach the minor road. Turn right, to reach your starting point in only 500m.

61. BEN HIANT HOLY HILL (528M/1,731FT)

MAP	OS SHEET 47 (GR 537632)
DISTANCE	10KM
ASCENT	530M
TIME	4–5 HRS
ACCESS	DESCRIBED CIRCULAR ROUTE: VIEWPOINT CAR PARK (GR 563617)
	DIRECT ROUTE, LINEAR: OLD QUARRY (GR 551641)
DIFFICULTY	COASTAL APPROACH AND STEEP GRASSY ASCENT; RETURN PATH
SUMMARY	Ben Hiant is the highest point of Ardnamurchan, Scotland's most westerly mainland peninsula. It is also, quite simply, one of Scotland's finest wee coastal hills, having cracking views and a rugged character – a mountain in miniature.

BEN HIANT'S HOLY connections are likely to derive from Cladh Chiarain (the graveyard of Ciarain), situated at Camus nan Geall (white bay). St Ciarain, was actually buried in Ireland in the 6th century AD. The site was dedicated to him by St Columba on a pilgrimage north from Iona.

Ben Hiant, Beinn na Seilg and the great tertiary ring complex centred on Glen Drian were sites of immense

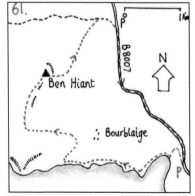

volcanic activity some 50 million years ago, and the retreat of ice some 8,000 years ago has left a boreal and a profoundly beautiful landscape of polished, ice-scoured, bare rock pushing through the moraine, now mellowed by a green carpet of vegetation.

I believe Ben Hiant to be worth more than a quick up and down from the highest point on the road and so the described route begins at the fine little viewpoint above the silver strand of Camus nan Geall, where there is a good view of Ben Hiant. The route follows the coastline for about 2.5km, before ascending the hill and returning by the direct route and road.

Park in the large parking area overlooking Camus nan Geall, just off the B8007 from Salen to Kilchoan and Ardnamurchan Point.

Follow the track which winds down to the beach. Continue along the coastal path, out to the point of Sgeir

Ben Hiant

Fhada where there are remains of an Iron Age fort. The path becomes less distinct from here and ends at the area known as Port a'chamais, 1km short of the prominent headland known as Maclean's Nose, really the end of the curving south spur of Ben Hiant.

Head inland at this point, through a grassy hollow, with the option of visiting the ruined village of Bourblaige in a hidden valley ahead. Gradually turn south-west to ascend steeper slopes onto a series of shoulders and small knolls.

At this point, there are two options to reach the summit. The first moves onto the knoll of Stallachan Dubha, before following the line of the mountain's south-west ridge over several knolls. The second moves right to ascend a grassy spur and upper slopes to arrive on the shoulder, just east of the summit. The first option explores more of the hill's character and is recommended.

The summit area has a trig point and cairn, with spectacular views along Loch Sunart and south to the island of Mull. In clear weather, the Skye Cuillin, Ben Nevis and many other mountains are all visible. The summit of Ben Hiant is a difficult place to leave on a summer's day!

Descend by the main summit path which winds round the seaward side of the summit, traversing a steep grassy slope. The path then follows the grassy crest of the hill's north-east ridge over several small knolls. There is a very fine view looking back to the

Summit of Ben Hiant

craggy summit promontory, which is not apparent from the top. The path continues easily to the road, where the old quarry parking area is visible on the opposite side.

Turn right at the road for a pleasant, 2.5km stroll back to the starting point at Camus nan Geall.

62. BEN LAGA HILL OF THE HOLLOW (512M/1679FT)

MAP	OS SHEET 40 (GR 645621)
DISTANCE	6KM
ASCENT	490M
TIME	2.5–4 HRS
ACCESS	LAGA (GR 633611)
DIFFICULTY	GENTLE, MAINLY PATHLESS ASCENT, STEEP DESCENT, CRAGGY OUTCROPS
SUMMARY	Ben Laga is a wonderfully wild and craggy little hill, rising steeply from the shore of Loch Sunart. It is the highest point in the eastern part of Ardnamurchan and gives magnificent views from its rocky summit.

A HILL TRACK runs northwards from Laga to link with the Glenborrodale to Acharacle path near Loch Laga and is useful for climbing both Ben Laga and its northerly neighbour of Meall nan Each (both Marilyns). The walk described can easily be extended to include Meall nan Each.

Park just west of the bridge over the Allt Laga and walk back over the bridge to reach the start of the hill track.

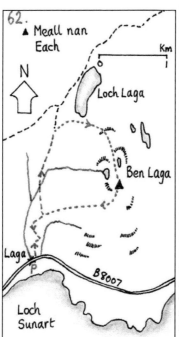

A new driveway to a house gives the initial impression of a private access, but a gate on the left, about 200m up the driveway leads to the hill track, which ascends the south-facing slope in a big dog-leg.

Higher up, the track degenerates into more of a rough path; follow it for about 2.5km to the vicinity of Loch Laga, just before the join with the Glenborrodale to Acharacle path. An easy ascent of Meall nan Each can be made from here if so wished.

Loch Sunart from Ben Laga

Turn right off the path and descend slightly to cross a small burn, before tackling the steep slope up to the well-defined and easy-angled north ridge of Ben Laga. Ascend this ridge, weaving around the various outcrops, to reach a series of lochans just below the final summit crag. This is a beautifully wild spot. Continue onwards to the summit cairn, which is perched on a big rock slab, with wonderful views along Loch Sunart. The massive cone of Beinn Resipol is very prominent to the east.

The descent can be varied by following a roughly south-westerly direction from the summit, past Lochan Coire na Moine, on a shoulder of the hill. There follows a steep descent back to the ascent track above the dog-leg. There is no well-defined route here, however, and you may wish to return by the route of ascent.

63. MEALL AN T-SLAMAIN (467M/1,531FT)

MAP	OS SHEET 41 (GR 070739)
DISTANCE:	7KM
ASCENT	480M
TIME	3–4 HRS
ACCESS	CAMASNAGAUL (GR 095751)
DIFFICULTY	GENTLE, GRASSY, BUT PATHLESS ASCENT
SUMMARY	This hill totally dominates the view across Loch Linnhe from Fort William and commands an unparalleled panorama of Ben Nevis and north-east up the Great Glen.

STANDING ON THE northern edge of the Great Glen Fault line, this hill gives a superb appreciation of the geography and geology of the region. It is rarely climbed, owing to its isolated position opposite the 'outdoor capital' of Scotland, but access is simplified by a passenger ferry from Fort William to Camusnagaul on the opposite side of the loch.

The derivation of the name is unclear but is possibly a corruption of the Gaelic 'slinnean', meaning 'shoulder-blade' – the hill has a long north-eastern spur with several level shoulders that form the route of ascent.

The start of the ascent route and Camusnagaul can be reached by car by a circuitous route round Loch Eil or by use of the Corran Ferry over Loch Linnhe, but if you are based in Fort William it makes sense to use the passenger ferry for a return fee of only £3. The ferry leaves from the small pier on the sea-front,

where there is also a tea-room and restaurant. At the time of writing, a boat leaves at 12.20 pm and returns at 4.20 pm, giving nearly 4 hours to complete the ascent. The crossing time is 10 minutes.

From the jetty at Camusnagaul, turn right along the minor road, crossing a cattle grid before heading left, upwards through woodland on a slightly overgrown but signposted trail. This path climbs steadily before contouring round the hillside. Follow it to a fence and gate, before leaving the trail directly up open hillside above the trees.

A fairly steep, tussocky ascent takes

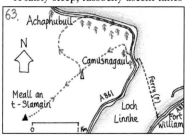

Meall an t-Slamain

you to the broad, grassy ridge where there is a radio mast and trig point at an altitude of 291m. In clear weather, there will already be excellent views across to Fort William backed by the massive bulk of 'The Ben'. The new track leading northwards downhill from the mass is a good descent route.

From the mast and trig point it is simply a matter of following the ridge-line south-westward by a series of steepenings and shoulders to the summit cairn. You should pass two smaller cairns set on shoulders en route to the actual top, which is set back slightly from the steep, south-eastern flank of the hill.

As already noted, the summit is a marvellous viewpoint and gives one of the finest views of Ben Nevis.

The descent can be varied by following the new mast access track down to Achaphubuil where there are fine views of the sawmill across the Corpach Narrows. Turn right at the road and walk for about 1.5km to reach the jetty at Camasnagaul.

Ben Nevis and Fort William from Meall an t-Slamain

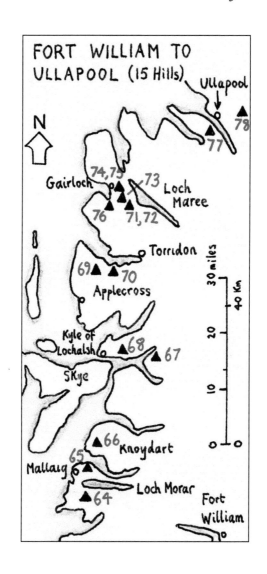

64. SIDHEAN MOR BIG FAIRY HILL (601M/1,972FT)

MAP	OS SHEET 40 (GR 729866)
DISTANCE	8KM
ASCENT	540M
TIME	3–4.5 HRS
ACCESS	A830 AT BEASDALE BURN (GR 716853)
DIFFICULTY	EASY VALLEY APPROACH WITH RUGGED, PATHLESS ASCENT AND DESCENT
SUMMARY	Sidhean Mor is the highest point of the wild area south of Loch Morar and west of the River Meoble. This is a region riddled with hill lochans and ice-scoured slabs, with great potential for much exploratory rambling.

THE DESCRIBED ROUTE is a short, circular tour, beginning with a walk along peaceful Glen Beasdale, but a longer circuit is possible using the Borrodale Path, west of the hill, and this is also mentioned briefly.

Fort William to Mallaig is considered by many to be the most scenic drive in Scotland and on a clear, sunny day it would be hard to disagree with this assertion.

Begin at a sharp bend in the road, about 1km north of Loch nan Uamh, where the Prince's Cairn is situated. Park at the lay-by just after the road goes under the railway bridge and walk north for 200m to the point where the main road swings left. Go through a metal gate on the right and follow

the path, which passes through a wooded area and crosses a stream into Glen Beasdale. The steep and partly wooded slopes on the left rise up to Sidhean Mor, the summit of which is hidden beyond the ridge. Glen Beasdale is well endowed with fine deciduous woods, especially on its southern side, and the whole glen has a tranquil air. If it is late spring, you will no doubt hear a cuckoo heralding

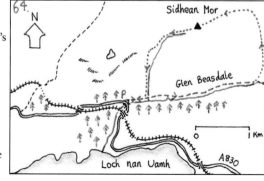

Glen Beasdale

the start of summer.

The path becomes sketchy at a grassy, level part of the glen, but soon materialises again after a gap in a dry stone wall. Several 'runrig' corrugations in the ground are evidence that this Highland glen was once inhabited; like many others, it is now deserted. In the upper part of the glen, the path climbs and traverses along the lower slopes of Sidhean Mor, and seems to disappear well before the point it supposedly reaches on the map.

At this point it should be noted that another hill (Beinn nan Cabar) lies almost 4km east of Sidhean Mor and will no doubt be of interest to Marilyn-baggers (both this and Sidhean Mor are Marilyns). The main advantage of this route is that Beinn

nan Cabar can also be included in the round, but will add at least another two hours onto the time. Sidhean Mor is the superior summit, however, with finer views.

The terrain between the two hills is very complex, with many knolls, ridges and outcrops and good map-reading is required to find the route with the minimum amount of ascent and descent.

To tackle Sidhean Mor singly, turn off the path at almost any point in the upper glen, or when the path disappears, and climb the easier-angled slopes of the south-eastern aspect of the hill. As you gain height, gradually swing round from north to west until you reach the rocky summit ridge. The cairn stands perched on a prominent

View from Sidhean Mor

craggy knoll in a delightfully airy position, with stunning sea views of the Small Isles, with the Sgurr of Eigg and the Rum Cuillin dominating the western skyline and further north, the 'antlered Cuillin' of Skye rise in saw-toothed splendour. This must be one of the finest viewpoints in Western Scotland.

About 100m away on another little knoll, is the trig point, 2m lower than the cairn.

The quickest descent involves taking a roughly western line from the summit, gradually descending on a series of easy grassy ramps, avoiding the crags. After about 1km, drop left into a depression, just before an obvious conical knoll on the ridge. This leads down fairly steep, grassy slopes to the right of a wooded gully with a stream, and arrives on the glen floor near an old stone sheep fank, visible from above. Reach the path, and then turn right along it to arrive back at the road. If you are not happy descending steep slopes, then continue west on the summit ridge until you reach the Borrodale path, where you turn left to reach the road, about 2km west of the starting point.

A much longer circuit can be made by walking up the Borrodale Path as far as Carn a'Mhadaidh-ruaidh and then traversing the high ground in a wide arc round Loch a'Choire Riabhaich on to the summit. This route gives a good appreciation of the area's wild scenery.

65. SGURR AN EILEIN GHIUBHAIS PEAK OF THE ISLAND OF THE FIR (522M/1,713FT)

MAP	OS SHEET 40 (GR 727973)
DISTANCE	13KM
ASCENT	700M
TIME	4–6 HRS
ACCESS	GLASNACARDOCH (GR 676957)
DIFFICULTY	GOOD APPROACH TRACK THEN EXTREMELY RUGGED, PATHLESS TERRAIN
SUMMARY	Sgurr an Eilein Ghiubhais is a coastal hill par excellence – remote, rocky and totally dominated by sea vistas in all directions, particularly across to Knoydart and Skye. This hill has a distinctive maritime ambience which is hard to beat.

THIS CRAGGY EMINENCE lies on the western extremity of the narrow piece of land between Loch Morar and Loch Nevis and is seen to advantage from the remote, land-locked village of Inverie in Knoydart, where it dominates the view across Loch Nevis. It is actually the smaller, north-easterly neighbour of the Marilyn Carn a'Ghobhair, but commands finer views, especially northwards across

Loch Nevis. Its name derives from the small islet to the north, Eilein Ghiubhais.

Begin at the small settlement of Glasnacardoch, a mile south of Mallaig, where cars can be parked near the junction of the A830 on a minor road. There is a signpost indicating the footpath to Loch an Nostarie and Loch Eireagoraidh, the latter lying just south of the Marilyn summit which is climbed en route to Sgurr an Eilein Ghiubhais.

Follow the signposted route along a tarmac lane under the railway line and past a few houses, before going through a gate to

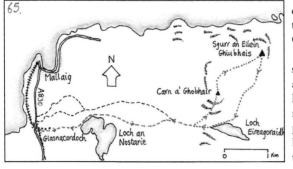

Sgurr an Eilein Ghiubhais from Inverie

a well-made cycle path, which reaches Loch an Nostarie in 1km. From here, a gate leads to an unmade, boggy walking trail which skirts the loch for a short distance before gradually ascending eastwards for over 2km to a narrow pass between Carn a'Ghobhair and the steep, craggy north face of Carn Mhic a'Ghille-chaim.

During this section, the rocky prow of Carn a'Ghobhair dominates the scene and the route of ascent takes a line directly upwards, with plenty

Loch an Nostarie

Inverie from Sgurr an Eilein Ghiubhais

of scrambling opportunities if so desired. The summit has no cairn, but take time to admire the views. Eigg and Rum are very prominent to the south-west. Sgurr an Eilein Ghiubhais is very obvious, standing just over 1km away to the north-east. The north-east side of the hill you are on is quite steep and it is advisable to head northwards along the summit ridge until an easy descent can be made to reach fairly flat terrain peppered with the odd lochan and small knolls.

This is wild country with no paths other than deer-trails. Eagles, both golden and white-tailed, are worth looking out for. On reaching the slopes of the prime hill, gradually tend left up massive rock slabs and head for the left-hand (higher) of

two obvious summits separated by a gorge containing a small lochan. A good cairn marks the summit of this marvellous wee hill.

The panorama to the north and east is absolutely breath-taking, with Knoydart's grand Munros and Corbetts holding centre-stage above sheltered Inverie Bay across Loch Nevis. Skye and the Small Isles complete an idyllic scene. This is a summit which is difficult to leave.

The best return route is to descend southwards to Loch Eireagoraidh, picking up the path at its western end, leading back to the starting point. Note that the main peak south of this loch is Sgurr Bhuidhe (a Marilyn) and you may wish to include this as part of the round.

66. DRUIM NA CLUAIN-AIRIGHE RIDGE OF THE SUMMER SHIELING (518M/1,699FT)

MAP	OS SHEET 33 (GR 752035)
DISTANCE	9KM
ASCENT	518M
TIME	2–3 HRS
ACCESS	INVERIE, KNOYDART (GR 764002)
DIFFICULTY	FOREST TRACK, THEN PATHLESS, PART-CRAGGY ASCENT
SUMMARY	Though perhaps dwarfed by its more popular and illustrious Munro and Corbett neighbours, this wee hill nevertheless possesses a charm and remoteness, with a unique flavour of the fabled Knoydart peninsula.

THE REAL CHARM of this hill lies in its isolated position in the west of Scotland's remotest mainland peninsula. The area's only settlement at Inverie can be accessed by a half-hour boat trip from Mallaig or a 25km trek from Kinloch Hourn. While the crowds will be heading for one or more of Knoydart's three Munros and three Corbetts, you will be almost sure of meeting no-one on this hidden gem of a hill.

From the pier at Inverie, turn right towards the village and turn left almost immediately up a new cycle track leading to a forestry track higher up. Go left here and follow the track northwards through the forest to reach a gate at the forest boundary.

Go through the gate and continue northwards along the track on relatively level terrain with the steep grassy slopes of Beinn Bhreac rising up on your left. Another forest

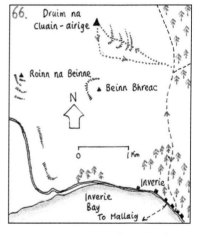

plantation appears on the right after 1km. Just past a track junction on the right, leave the track on the left and head slightly north of west, parallel to a fence, across initially boggy ground to reach the craggy eastern flank of the hill. Some scrambling is possible on the numerous rough crags

Druim na Cluain-airighe

and there is a succession of false tops before the true summit is reached – a cairn perched on a rocky plinth.

In clear weather, the summit views are delectable. Eastwards, there is a fine prospect of Scotland's most westerly mainland Munro, Ladhar Bheinn. To the west lies Skye and the iconic skyline of the Cuillin ridge. This is a summit to savour, steeping yourself in Knoydart's magic.

It is possible to make a circular tour by heading south-west along the knobbly spine of the ridge to Roinn na Beinne then descending to the Airor road and back to Inverie. However, the descent from this last peak is very steep, craggy and choked with bracken lower down. It is therefore advisable to return by the route of ascent, avoiding the crags on the south side.

View from Druim na Cluain-airghe

67. BEINN A'MHEADHOIN MIDDLE HILL (414M/1,358FT)

MAP	OS SHEET 33 (GR918288)
DISTANCE	8KM
ASCENT	470M
TIME	2.5–4 HRS
ACCESS	PUBLIC ROAD END (GR 897277)
DIFFICULTY	FAIRLY EASY GRASSY ASCENT WITH AVOIDABLE CRAGS
SUMMARY	This highly distinctive hill with its numerous humps, bumps and craggy cliffs is very prominent from the village of Dornie, and its ascent gives stunning views down Loch Long and Loch Alsh to Skye.

THIS WEE HILL never fails to catch the eye on the drive across Dornie Bridge, its complex and inviting topography tempting the keen hillwalker.

Park at the end of the minor road just over a mile from Dornie on the south side of Loch Long. A hill path goes east from here to Glen Elchaig, part of which is the return route.

Cross the bridge over the River Glennan and turn right, where you almost immediately start ascending the grassy west ridge of Beinn a'Mheadhoin. Very little height is gained before the view down Loch Long to Dornie and beyond begins to open out. Higher up, the ridge becomes more craggy and less well-defined and a multitude of possible routes present themselves.

The ridge levels off at an area of small knolls, with a little lochan (Loch Dubhach) nestling in a hollow behind the summit. The actual summit, on a grassy knoll with a small cairn, is a

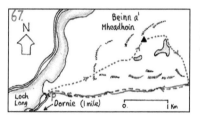

stupendous viewpoint. The obvious big hill to the south is Carn Bad a'Chreamha (a Graham Top) and well worth an ascent.

The large lochan east of the summit shares the same name as the hill and is the next objective. Descend easily

Beinn a' Mheadhoin from Dornie

View from Beinn a' Mheadhoin

to the northern arm of the lochan and enjoy the tranquillity, before following its shoreline on the eastern side. Go up an obvious depression away from the lochan and head in a roughly southern direction over dips and hollows, before descending steeply to the hill path mentioned previously.

Turn right and follow the path pleasantly through the steep-sided glen by the River Glennan for about 3.5km back to your starting point.

68. AUCHTERTYRE HILL (453M/1,486FT)

MAP	OS SHEET 33 (GR 832289)
DISTANCE	6KM
ASCENT	430M
TIME	2–3 HRS
ACCESS	BALMACARA SQUARE (GR 806284)
DIFFICULTY	FOREST TRACK AND STEEP ASCENT; SOME LOOSE ROCK
SUMMARY	The steep and craggy western profile of this hill presents a distinctive backdrop to the village of Balmacara and its ascent offers a wide-ranging panorama to Skye and the mountains of the western seaboard.

AUCHTERTYRE HILL IS the highest point of the Balmacara Estate lying north of Loch Alsh and south of the model village of Plockton at Loch Carron. Access to the hill from Balmacara Square has become easier in recent years with the construction of new forestry tracks and trails, but still involves a fairly steep ascent to the summit area.

It is possible to ascend the hill from the A899 Stromeferry road to the east, involving much less ascent, but it is tussocky and trackless, with no appreciation of the hill's fine western profile.

Balmacara Square, lying less than a mile north of the A87 Kyle of Lochalsh road, has a visitor centre and plenty of parking space. Follow the sign for 'Forest Trails' along the tarmac road and over the bridge. Ignore the footpath sign and instead turn left along a vehicle track which gradually ascends through the forest.

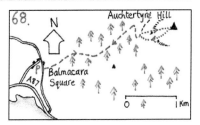

After about 1km there is a grand view of the hill's craggy western flank. Continue onwards until the track makes a couple of hairpin bends and you find yourself directly beneath the steep slopes.

A small cairn marks the start of a faint path which climbs directly upwards to enter a gap between two rocky prows. There is the possibility of scrambling on the left prow, but be warned – the rock is loose in places. The ground further right is slightly less steep and marks the route of descent.

At the summit plateau, head west through a mass of bog cotton and ascend further minor crags to reach the

Auchtertyre Hill

summit trig point perched on a rocky platform. The views in all directions are very fine, especially west over to the Skye Cuillin. This would be a marvellous place to appreciate a West Highland sunset.

Descend largely by the route of ascent, avoiding the crags below the summit plateau by moving to their left.

View from Auchtertyre Hill

69. CROIC-BHEINN HILL OF THE DEER'S ANTLER (494M/1,620FT)

MAP	OS SHEET 24 (GR 762518)
DISTANCE	11KM
ASCENT	470M
TIME	3–4.5 HRS
ACCESS	INVERBAIN (GR 787549)
DIFFICULTY	REASONABLE APPROACH TRACK AND EASY, GRASSY ASCENT
SUMMARY	Croic-bheinn's detached aloofness of the northern half of the Applecross peninsula, with its northern arc of crags, give it an air of mystique which will be hard to resist for the mountain connoisseur.

CROIC-BHEINN IS ONE of those hills that really catches your attention when glancing at the map – it looks like a proper hill. Having an all-round drop of 123m (over 400ft), it doesn't make it to the list of Marilyns, but it cries out to be climbed.

The best approach is from Inverbain, on the Applecross coastal road and about 6km from Shieldaig. From here, an old right of way takes a natural line through the hills to the village of Applecross, a distance of about 13km and a fine walk. The route to Croic-bheinn uses part of this old path. Just north of the bridge at Inverbain there is a small parking area and a sign saying '8 miles to Applecross'.

Walk up the track opposite, which goes to a cottage, before turning right

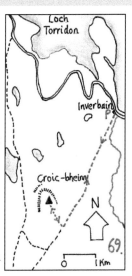

to follow the steep wooded slopes above the Abhainn Dubh (Black River). Both this path and the one to Kenmore, further along the coast, are old coffin routes dating back 1,000 years, which were used by burial parties from northern settlements, heading for the burial ground at Clachan Church in Applecross. There has been much recent tree planting around here, the aim, at least partly, to try and recreate the original forest which emerged following the last Ice Age. The most common trees planted are birch and Scots Pine.

Beyond a gate, the path becomes quite sketchy, but the route ahead is quite obvious, heading for a cairn at

Summit of Croic-bheinn

the top of a small rise. Between here and another cairn further on, the going can be quite boggy in places, with the path very intermittent, but the route continues to take a natural line up the wide depression. Finally, reach the second, more substantial cairn at a broad bealach (height 371m).

Leave the path at this point (just as it becomes more well-defined!) and head in a north-westerly direction to gradually gain the broad south ridge of the hill, where you head north. Higher up, the angle eases and you will soon encounter an increasing number of huge sandstone slabs and erratics, large freestanding boulders left when the last vestiges of ice disappeared around 8,000 years ago.

The true summit is marked by a large cairn and is about 300m south-west of the stone trig point, which is 1m lower in height. Not surprisingly, the summit panorama is magnificent, with the best views to the north-east,

where the jagged crests of the Torridon peaks steal the show. Closer at hand, the wee hill of Ben Shieldaig (a Hugh) is very prominent above the tiny row of cottages marking Shieldaig village.

The descent is more or less the route of ascent, but for those wanting a longer day out, it is easily possible to descend to the path on the west side of the hill and follow this northwards to Kenmore, a distance of some 6km. This is a more well-defined path, but longer than the approach path. The only disadvantage is that you will then have another 5km road walk to reach Inverbain. However, being a quiet minor road with superb views, this may not be such a hardship.

If you decide to return by the ascent route, do not try to take a shortcut east to the path, as there is a line of steep sandstone crags blocking the way.

70. BEN SHIELDAIG (530M/1,739FT)

MAP	OS SHEET 24 (GR 833524)
DISTANCE	8KM
ASCENT	530M
TIME	2.5–4 HRS
ACCESS	BALGY BRIDGE (GR 847543)
DIFFICULTY	MAINLY ROUGH AND PATHLESS WITH SOME STEEP SECTIONS
SUMMARY	Steep-sided Ben Shieldaig totally dominates the picturesque and sheltered seaside village of the same name and offers an unrivalled panorama across Loch Torridon to Beinn Alligin and the other Torridonian giants.

THE NAME SHIELDAIG most likely derives from the Norse '*sild-vig*', meaning Herring Bay and, indeed, like Ullapool, the pretty settlement of Shieldaig was built as a planned fishing village in the early 1800s, with herring providing much of its early trade.

Ben Shieldaig towers above the village in tiers of sandstone, its craggy ramparts looking almost impenetrable. In fact, the hill's long, knobbly summit ridge, guarded on all sides by relentlessly steep slopes with no paths, has very few chinks in its armour. In spite of the hill's formidable steep defences, its ascent rewards the determined hillwalker with one of the most sublime views in Scotland.

The gentlest route up Ben Shieldaig is from the southern end of its long summit ridge, but this is far from the actual top and would require a return by the same route or a steep descent followed by a road-walk. In contrast, the hill can be ascended by

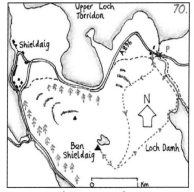

its steep and craggy north-western spur, directly from Shieldaig village, but this involves some intimidating situations and is not recommended.

The described route begins just east of Balgy Bridge on the A896 road, where there is limited parking near the start of a walking trail to Annat. Walk west over the bridge and turn off the road to the left at a stone outhouse. A rough track heads south-west to Loch Damh from here. Follow this track

Ben Shieldaig across Loch Shieldaig

until it crosses a small stream after several hundred metres and then leave the track, heading roughly south-west to the craggy, undulating shoulder on your right.

The terrain is quite tussocky and boggy until you reach firmer ground at the shoulder, where the going is easier on pockets of glaciated gneiss slabs. Gradually turn south through a complex area of knolls, spurs and rock outcrops until you reach a wide, grassy corrie facing the north end of Loch Damh.

Ascend easy, grass slopes in the corrie until you reach the col on Ben Shieldaig's summit ridge at GR 838518. From here, the summit is less than 1km distant, up and along the ridge in a north-westerly direction. The cairn

sits on a rock slab and overlooks the beautiful summit lochan of Loch nan Eun (loch of the birds) where you may well spot a red- or black-throated diver.

On a clear day, it is the Torridonian pair of Munros across Loch Torridon that arrest the eye like no other mountains in Scotland. The ice-sculpted, angular, yet elegant profile of Beinn Alligin and the castellated, sandstone battlements of Liathach are seen to perfection from this unique vantage point. Closer at hand, to the east, across Loch Damh, is the graceful ridge of the Corbett, Beinn Damh.

Take time to absorb the view and perhaps stroll round the loch. You may also wish to continue along the ridge for 800m to the trig point,

Summit lochan of Ben Shieldaig

which is lower and offers much the same view.

The return route can be slightly varied by returning to the corrie and descending directly to the shores of Loch Damh. A fairly recent fish farm and associated clutter have partly robbed this loch of its wild quality. Follow the shore of the loch to the end of the track and walk along the track for a pleasant final kilometre to the road and your starting point.

Torridon from Ben Shieldaig

71. MEALL A'GHLAS LEOTHAID HILL OF GREY SLOPES
(342M/1,122FT)
72. MEAL LOCHAN A'CHLEIRICH HILL OF THE LOCH OF THE CLERIC
(403M/1322 FT)

MAP	OS SHEET 19 (GR 863707, 872716)
DISTANCE	6KM
ASCENT	440M
TIME	2.5–4 HRS
ACCESS	RED STABLE PARKING AREA, A832 (GR 857722)
DIFFICULTY	MAINLY ROUGH AND PATHLESS WITH NUMEROUS CRAGS
SUMMARY	These two marvellous, craggy wee hills are seen to advantage on the A832 road near Am Feur-Loch (Loch of the Grassy Pasture) and their combined ascent gives a superb walk with wonderful views of mountain and loch.

THE REGION OF Flowerdale, north of Torridon, has a host of minor summits composed almost entirely of Lewisian Gneiss, a beautifully hard and rough rock that makes for excellent scrambling and walking. These two peaks, in particular the higher one, are commonly ignored by the Corbett-bagging masses, their hearts set on the bigger prizes of Baosbheinn and Beinn an Eoin.

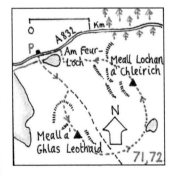

The small parking area at the Red Stable, a corrugated-iron building (now painted green) on the A382 west of Loch Maree, is the usual starting point for the long walk-in to the aforementioned Corbetts. It is also the site of the tranquil Am Feur-Loch, where there is a grand view of Meall Lochan a'Chleirich, a hill which begs to be climbed, thrusting skywards in castellated tiers of rough Lewisian Gneiss.

The described route climbs this hill after Meall a'Ghlas Leothaid, but could just as easily be reversed. Begin by following the obvious footpath over the bridge. Just ahead on the right is a small shelter with information about the area. Throughout the walk you will come across many recently planted Scots Pine, the work of Gairloch Estate. There is mention of the 'trail' up the

Meall Lochan a' Chleirich

first hill, marked by wooden posts and signalled blue on the shelter map.

The path climbs steadily onto the northern spur of Meall a'Ghlas Leothaid and you will need to keep your eyes peeled for a small path going off to the right just under 1km from the start. At the time of writing this was marked only by a piece of duckboard. The path up the hill is unmade and marked by posts about every 100m. It takes a rough line up the northern spur to reach the flattish summit ridge, where you traverse one small knoll before reaching the actual summit, marked by a stone view indicator.

On a clear day, this is a grand spot to just stare and reflect on the surrounding panorama, a stunning array of peaks and lochs in one of Scotland's finest areas.

To descend, follow the posts south-eastwards along the summit ridge and

Summit of Meall a Ghlas Leothaid

Summit of Meall Lochan a'Chleirich

down to a grassy col, where the faint path turns to drop down to the main trail. Cross over the trail and make a bee-line for Lochan a'Chleirich, across rather tussocky, pathless terrain. This little lochan nestles under the southern flank of the hill from which it takes its name.

Cross a small stream connecting the lochan to a smaller one and begin climbing the hill through pockets of new Scots Pine trees. There is one steep section higher up, which can be avoided by turning right into a depression. The angle soon eases and the summit cairn on a rocky plinth is quickly reached.

The view from here is even better than the first hill, as it stands directly above the magnificent, island-studded Loch Maree, perhaps the most beautiful of all Scottish lochs. The view east across the loch to the arrow-head of Slioch is simply breath-taking. Southwards, the twin Corbetts of Baosbheinn and Beinn an Eoin steal the show.

Descend the hill in a generally north-western direction, avoiding the massive buttresses and crags by easy, grassy ramps. Ascending this side of the hill would allow small pockets of scrambling, but the rock is not as continuous or easy-angled as it looks from below. Reach a wide grassy gully and follow it by a burn to Am Feur-Loch, where you turn right by a deer fence.

Unfortunately, this fence makes a right-angled turn just before the road and you will need to climb it in order to reach the road. Turn left and return to the starting point in a few hundred metres.

73. MEALL AUNDRARY (327M/1,073FT)

MAP   OS SHEET 19 (GR 846728)

DISTANCE   4KM

ASCENT   210M

TIME   1.5–2 HRS

ACCESS: RED STABLE PARKING AREA, A832 (GR 857722)

DIFFICULTY   EASY, GRASSY ASCENT WITH OPTIONAL SCRAMBLING

SUMMARY   This is the most southerly of the fine rocky peaks in the wild area to the north-west of Loch Maree and to the east of the A832. It provides an ideal short outing with some scrambling and terrific views.

FOR MEALL AUNDRARY, use the same parking area as for the two hills to the south-east (see Routes 71–72). From here, an obvious track leaves to the east of the parking area and heads north-west in the direction of the hill. Unfortunately, it ends in just a few hundred metres, but a rough all-terrain vehicle track can still be followed, heading directly for the slabby south-east spur of the hill.

A distinctive ribbon of easy-angled

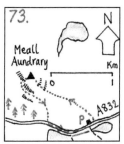

gneiss slabs is very obvious and provides an entertaining wee scramble. These can be avoided on the right if so wished. Above here, follow easy terrain to the first of two distinct summits, both about the same height. The second one has a small cairn and is reached by a steep descent to a tiny lochan, followed by a further rocky climb to the top.

There is a very fine view north

Meall Aundrary

Sidhean Mor and An Groban from Meall Aundrary

to the twin summits of Sidhean Mor and An Groban (see Routes 74–75) and the panorama of Torridon giants to the south and south-east is magnificent.

Descend south-west from the summit and follow a long grassy ramp south-eastwards, before turning south into a grassy depression which brings you onto the A832 in only about 20 minutes. Turn left and follow the road for less than 1km to the parking area.

74. AN GROBAN POINT OF ROCK (383M/1,257FT)
75. SIDHEAN MOR BIG FAIRY HILL (384M /1,260FT)

MAP	OS SHEET 19 (GR 838750, 836740)
DISTANCE	9KM
ASCENT	570M
TIME	3.5–5 HRS
ACCESS	OLD INN, CHARLESTOWN, GAIRLOCH (GR 811752)
DIFFICULTY	EASY APPROACH TRACK FOLLOWED BY ROUGH, CRAGGY TERRAIN AND INTERMITTENT PATHS
SUMMARY	These two rocky gems, but especially An Groban, embody the very essence of the nature of the term, Hugh. Rocky, rugged and romantic, these two twins, born of Lewisian Gneiss, possess more character than many a mountain twice or even three times their height.

LYING NORTH AND west of Loch Maree and to the east of Gairloch is a huge 40 square km area of countless rocky knolls, hills and lochans. Apart from a right-of-way trail from Slattadale in the south to Tollie in the north, at the extreme east of the area, there are very few walking routes into this relatively unfrequented wild landscape. The highest point (Meall an Doirein) is a Marilyn, but has nowhere near the charm and individuality of An Groban.

Begin near the 'Old Inn' in Charlestown where there is a parking area on the right just beyond the bridge. Walk up the path to the right of the vehicle track going to Flowerdale House. This path is signposted to Flowerdale Waterfall, which is passed en route to the hill.

Flowerdale Estate has been the seat of the Mackenzie Clan since 1494 and the name 'Flowerdale' was coined by the 9th laird, Alexander Mackenzie, who was impressed with the amount and variety of wild flowers in the area.

The rocky façade of An Groban is visible from the start of the walk and is a fine backdrop to the river and peaceful harbour.

The initial path is well signposted and meanders its way through the

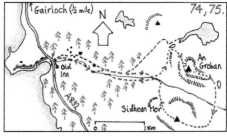

An Groban

grounds of the estate over several bridges and boardwalk areas. At the time of writing, a new Hydro Scheme was in the process of construction and there was the odd diversion. Beyond Flowerdale Mains join the main track and continue upwards until a smaller track forks off to the right. Take this path and cross a wooden footbridge constructed by Royal Engineers.

Beyond the bridge, the path narrows and becomes steep and slippery as it climbs up to the top of the waterfall. A short distance further on, you will emerge from tree cover and reach another wooden footbridge crossing the stream on your right. There is an excellent view of An Groban from here, rising up to the left in tiered buttresses and aprons of gneiss, giving an air of impregnability. For those with a head for heights and some scrambling ability there are some fine routes to the summit on the broad area of easier angled slabs further on. For more details, consult the Scottish Mountaineering Club guide *Highland Scrambles North*.

For the pedestrian however, there is an easier and devious route following a series of grassy shelves and ramps. From the upper bridge do not take the path heading directly up the glen, but turn left along another path following a line of wooden posts. This path ascends tussocky slopes to cross a deer fence by a stile, about 200m above another stile. The path continues less distinctly up a broad, grassy ramp on the left with a massive rock wall on

Summit of An Groban

the right.

Descend slightly to reach a small dam and concrete weir, part of the recent Hydro Scheme using the outflow of Loch Airigh a'Phuill on the north side of An Groban. Continue to follow the wooden posts up a rocky outcrop to a small cairn, where there is a fine view of the north buttresses of the hill.

At this point, the path descends towards the loch and you should head off to the right over a slabby section on a faint path which soon leads onto the main spine of the hill, below a low crag. A short, but easy, scramble ascends an obvious weakness in the crag, leading to a flatter section. The path continues onwards into an open, grassy gully with a flattened cairn at

its foot. Ascend the gully, easily, and then swing right at the top to reach a small shoulder, where you turn left below a steep wall on a grassy terrace. The path turns right again to a level area just below the summit and a short, steeper section takes you to the stone trig point on a rocky plinth.

Not surprisingly, the panorama from this craggy perch is stunning, dominated by sea views to the north-west and the Torridon Munros to the south-east.

Your second hill of the day, Sidhean Mor, stands only 1km away, across the glen, but will require a circuitous route to reach.

Go south-east along An Groban's summit ridge, past a tiny lochan, and gradually descend to a high, grassy

View west from An Groban

col on the ridge. Do not try to leave the ridge yet, but continue onwards over the next rise to a relatively flat section, before descending leftwards to the vicinity of a small lochan. From here, descend easy tussocky terrain, gradually turning southwards before a waterfall, to go down a heathery gully and arrive at the flat, boggy, head of the glen.

If you wish to omit the second hill, it is an easy matter to just head down the glen and retrace your ascent route. There is no path onto Sidhean Mor, but follow the obvious line up its south-eastern spur, bypassing the odd crag to eventually arrive at the summit cairn, just 1m higher than An Groban.

From the summit, head north-west along the ridge to the obvious subsidiary top several hundred metres away. You will need to navigate an initial steep descent crag first. From this second top, descend easily into a broad, grassy gully, keeping left to avoid any crags. This takes you down to the floor of the glen, where you cross a stream to join the path through the glen. The return route can be varied by crossing the upper bridge and following a well-made trail through the woods on the south side of the main stream. You will pass a memorial to Iain Mackay, a blind piper of the 17th century. Turn right at a forestry track and then left to rejoin the ascent route.

76. SIDHEAN MOR BIG FAIRY HILL (225M/738FT)

MAP	OS SHEET 19 (GR 812716)
DISTANCE	3KM
ASCENT	220M
TIME	1.5–2.5 HRS
ACCESS	START OF SHIELDAIG TO TORRIDON PATH (GR 807724)
DIFFICULTY	MUDDY APPROACH PATH AND EASY GRASSY ASCENT, OPTIONAL SCRAMBLING
SUMMARY	A beautiful rocky wee peak offering an ideal summer evening's walk. Added extras include the tranquil Fairy Lochs and a visit to the crash site of an American war plane.

THIS FINE, CRAGGY SPIRE is well appreciated from the B8056 when driving east from the quaint seaside hamlet of Badachro. Despite its close proximity to this road, its situation just north of an idyllic scattering of hill lochans and its rocky profile give it a marvellous, wild character. A fine circuit can be made by also visiting the site of an American bomber crash during the Second World War.

Begin on the B8056 just over a mile from its junction with the A832 Gairloch road, where a walking right-of-way heads south to Torridon. This track is signposted as such.

Walk along the track (going through a gate) for a few hundred metres until you reach an unmade path forking off to the left at a wooded area. This was signposted 'Fairy Lochs Crash Site' at the time of writing. Follow this path upwards through a pocket of silver birch, beyond which you should see another similar sign to the crash site. The path becomes progressively muddier as you gain height, and the craggy northern top of Sidhean Mor soon comes into view.

Several other signs indicate the route up by a stream to a deer fence and kissing gate adjacent to the northernmost of the Fairy Lochs. Go through the gate and stay on the path as it climbs slightly, before swinging

Sidhean Mor from Fairy Lochs

to the left and descending to a smaller lochan on the right.

You will soon spot an Excalibur-like propeller blade rising from the waters of the loch and a second blade and engine parts scattered at the base of a steep crag, where a plaque gives details of the crash. The American Liberator Bomber was on its return to the USA when it crashed here in June 1945, killing all 15 airmen, crew and passengers, whose average age was

Summit of Sidhean Mor

View north-west from Sidhean Mor

only 21. It is thought that the aircraft hit the summit of Slioch, some 19km to the south-east, before gradually losing height to crash at this spot.

The site is fairly frequently visited, both by descendents of the crash victims and by the curious. There is a poignant peace around the whole area which is quite profound.

Return to the gate in the deer fence, but do not go through it. Instead, head eastwards, roughly following the edge of the loch and climb easy slopes until An Sidhean is visible ahead. Climb the rocky south-west face by any number of lines. The most sporting route moves to the right in the final stages to ascend a grand rib

of gneiss by a 10m scramble. The summit trig point has stupendous views in all directions, especially down to the sheltered harbour of Loch Shieldaig.

Descend north-west to a small grassy col, before turning left to drop down a steep heathery gully. Turn right for several hundred metres to reach a second gate in the deer fence. Go through this and continue downhill on a very rough path to rejoin the route of ascent.

On your return, a visit to the Badachro Inn is a must – not only to quench your thirst, but to drink in remembrance of the air-crash victims. The Inn is easily the finest in the area.

77. BEINN NAM BAN HILL OF THE WASTE LAND (580M/ 1,903FT)

MAP	OS SHEET 19 (GR 109908)
DISTANCE	4KM
ASCENT	340M
TIME	1.5–2.5 HRS
ACCESS	MINOR ROAD TO BADRALLOCH (GR 100919)
DIFFICULTY	TUSSOCKY GRASS AND ROCK OUTCROPS
SUMMARY	Beinn nam Ban occupies a strategic position between Little Loch Broom and Loch Broom. Its rugged character and wonderful views are the reward for a very short outing.

BEINN NAM BAN is one of three distinct hills situated on the Scoraig peninsula, the main one being the Graham of Beinn Ghobhlach to the north-west. This hill provides the shortest outing of the three and gives the finest bird's-eye view of the north-west Highland 'capital', Ullapool. A fine view of the hill can be had from here, across Loch Broom.

The hairpin bend on the Badralloch road at GR 100919 is the obvious starting point for the ascent of this hill, but recently, 'No Parking' signs have appeared, so you may have to park some distance from this point. On this extremely quiet, no-through road, discreet use of a passing place would probably not go amiss. The old track from the hairpin bend, descending to the coast at Loch Broom, used to

link with a passenger ferry across to Ullapool, but sadly this no longer operates. I used it back in 1989 in the course of a month's backpacking trip from the Mull of Kintyre to Cape Wrath.

There is no obvious route to the top of this hill, other than meandering upwards in a general south-easterly direction. The middle section is fairly steep, but the going is generally fine, on tussocky grass and sandstone outcrops. Towards the summit, the angle eases and there are many sandstone slabs which can be used to avoid the boggy bits. Pass a tiny lochan just before the summit, where there is a good-sized cairn.

On a clear day, the view to the north is absolutely stunning, with Ben Mor Coigach, Cul Beag and Cul Mor all standing proud. Ullapool

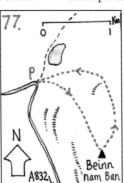

View North from Beinn nam Ban

itself is just hidden, but you will no doubt have seen it on the ascent, and will again on the descent. To the south, the jagged ridges of An Teallach are the prominent feature.

To avoid the steep middle section, and to gain a grand view of Ullapool, the descent can be varied by taking a line initially north-east and gradually swinging round in a big arc to the left (west) to eventually arrive back at the hairpin bend in the road.

Ullapool from Beinn nam Ban

78. MEALL LIATH CHOIRE HILL OF THE GREY CORRIE (548M/1,798FT)

MAP	OS SHEET 20 (GR 227962)
DISTANCE	24KM
ASCENT	530M
TIME	6–8 HRS
ACCESS	ULLAPOOL, A835 ROAD END (GR 128949)
DIFFICULTY	LONG, EASY APPROACH TRACK FOLLOWED BY ROUGH, PATHLESS TERRAIN
SUMMARY	A retiring and remote hill, hidden away in the lochan-studded hinterland of the Rhidorroch Forest, Meall Liath Choire is not a hill for the casual pedestrian, a bicycle would prove useful.

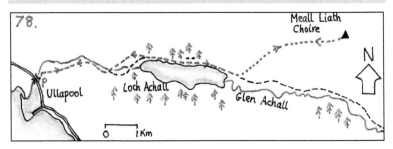

THIS HILL'S RELATIVE inaccessibility is part of its charm. The fact that it is situated north of Glen Achall, one of the most picturesque glens in Scotland (yet hardly known) only adds to its unique allure.

The route begins on the A835 north of Ullapool, just before the bridge over the Ullapool River where a minor road goes off to the right. Parking is quite restricted and you may need to consider leaving your car in Ullapool. The route to the foot of the hill follows an excellent vehicle track for 8km and a bike would be worth considering.

At the time of writing, the first kilometre or so of the track was taken over by construction vehicles and quarry machinery, but beyond, a peaceful ambience descends as you approach Loch Achall by any one of the two tracks which diverge and rejoin again at the loch.

The track along the north side of the loch gives glimpses of the intended peak and becomes increasingly wooded, with wonderful views across the glittering loch to tree-bound slopes on the opposite side. Pass the grounds of Rhidorroch House and continue onwards to the end of the loch.

Glen Achall

About 1km from the loch's end, leave the track and cross a level grassy section before ascending steep, grassy slopes to a second flat area containing a couple of lochans. Beyond here, the hill's ill-defined west ridge sweeps upwards over complex ground.

Climb this ridge by a variety of lines to reach a fairly level shoulder. The final ridge to the summit is more well-defined from here and you will pass a small lochan just before the last steepening to the summit cairn.

The feeling of isolation is quite profound on this far-flung peak and the view, especially to the north-west, is breath-taking. The Coigach peaks of Ben Mor Coigach, Stac Polly, Cul Beag, Cul Mor and Suilven are strung out along the horizon like pearls on a necklace.

Closer to home, 4km to the east is Cnoc Damh, another Marilyn, higher than Meall Liath Choire, but with less character. Determined baggers, however, will probably attempt these two together.

Return by the route of ascent.

Coigach from Meall Liath Choire

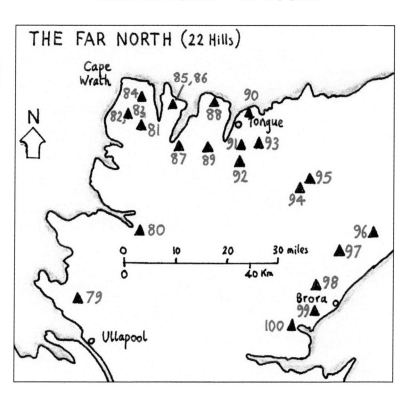

79. SGORR TUATH NORTH PEAK (588M/1,928FT)

MAP	OS SHEET 15 (GR 110075)
DISTANCE	10KM
ASCENT	680M
TIME	4–5 HRS
ACCESS	LOCH LURGAINN, SOUTH END (GR 138068)
DIFFICULTY	BOGGY PATH, THEN RUGGED RIDGE WALKING
SUMMARY	Sgorr Tuath is the slightly lower northern top of the Graham Beinn an Eoin (hill of the bird), in the heart of Coigach. The traverse of the southern top of Sgorr Deas (South Peak) is also included in the described route.

DESPITE ITS BEING 'just' the lower top of Beinn an Eoin, Sgorr Tuath has a distinctive character and shape from its slightly loftier neighbour and it is arguably the finer hill of the two.

Park on the minor road to Achiltibuie, about 2 miles from the A835, at the southern extremity of Loch Lurgainn. You may need to park further away than this point.

Follow a boggy path starting just east of the bridge, leading to the Allt Claonaidh, which is crossed to reach the lower slopes of Cioch Beinn an Eoin, the first minor peak of the circuit. Ascend steep heather and sandstone slabs to its summit, where there are grand views of Stac Pollaidh and Cul Beag to the north.

Continue along the grand promenade of mainly rough sandstone slabs and admire the huge, rocky prow of Sgurr an Fhidhleir just across lonely Lochan Tuath. Reach the summit of Beinn an Eoin, where

you gain a very fine view of Sgorr Tuath rising above its tiny bealach lochan, and beyond, the bristling pinnacled ridge of Stac Pollaid. The other Coigach peaks all stand out in splendid isolation.

Follow the summit ridge before descending to the right to reach the little lochan nestling in a hollow in the col. The final climb up Sgorr Tuath can be made as easy or entertaining as you like, the hardest line giving some easy scrambling on the numerous outcrops.

The summit ridge is split by a fissure. Beyond the summit, some sandstone pinnacles provide a foreground for the view north.

Descend south-east on easy,

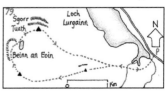

Sgorr Tuath and Stac Pollaidh beyond

heathery slopes and skirt round the northern flank of Cioch Beinn an Eoin to reach the route of ascent, which is followed back to the start.

80. STACK OF GLENCOUL (494M/1,621FT)

MAP	OS SHEET 15 (GR 290287)
DISTANCE	24KM
ASCENT	560M
TIME	6-8 HRS
ACCESS	A894, EAS A'CHUAL ALUINN FALLS PATH (GR 238284)
DIFFICULTY	LONG, SERIOUS, RUGGED APPROACH PATH THEN TUSSOCKY, PATHLESS GROUND
SUMMARY	This remote, awkwardly placed rocky tower possesses all the hallmarks of 'attitude'. Its character and romantic charm are undeniable, yet it is probably the least climbed of the classic small peaks in Scotland.

THE STACK OF GLENCOUL earns its 'stack status' courtesy of the view south-east along Loch Glencoul, from where it appears as a slender spire of rock rising from the craggy, watery wilderness of Assynt, one of the roughest and remotest areas of Scotland.

Landscape and geology go hand-in-hand here and Assynt contains a great variety of rock structures of exceptional international interest, one of which is the Stack of Glencoul. Standing bang on the edge of the fault

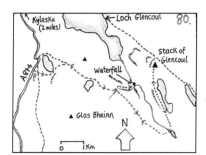

Stack of Glencoul

line known as the Moine Thrust, the hill is of significant geological importance.

The stack can be ascended by a variety of means and routes and is ideally placed for inclusion on a multi-day backpacking jaunt – the new Scottish National Trail passes very close by and there are also two mountain bothies, at Glencoul and Glendhu.

In the summer, there are boat trips from Kylesku to the head of Loch Glencoul in order to view Eas a'Chual

Eas a'Chual Aluinn Falls

Aluinn, 'The Beautiful Waterfall of the Niche' – the highest waterfall in Great Britain, with a vertical drop of 200m. The Falls are only about 1km south-west of the Stack and walkers can be dropped off at Glencoul. From there, it can be ascended easily, followed by a long walk out.

The described route, however, involves no backpacking or boats but uses the normal walkers' route to the Falls, followed by a mainly pathless dog-leg to reach the Stack.

Begin on the A894 road, 5 miles south of Kylesku, where a signpost indicates the path to the Eas a'Chual Aluinn Falls. Another path, beginning at the north end of Loch na Gainmhich joins the other path east of the loch and may also be used. Be aware that after very wet weather the outflow of the loch at its northern end may be swollen and uncrossable.

The path descends to the loch, before gradually climbing and crossing the Allt Loch Bealach a'Bhuirich to reach the loch of the same name in about 2.5km. This wild hill loch nestles in the bealach between Glas Bheinn and Cnoc na Creige and is a beautiful spot.

Beyond the loch, the Stack of Glencoul appears directly ahead, with the greater bulk of Beinn Leoid (a Corbett) beyond. Descend steeply for about 1km to reach the stream flowing down to the Falls. At this point, there is the option to follow the path to the left of the stream as it descends to the lip of the Falls in

Stack of Glencoul

less than 1km. It should be noted that although this gives close proximity to the Falls, you have a severely restricted view of them as you are only observing them from above and actually see very little.

The second option is to cross the stream about 20m to the right and continue on the main path as it contours along the rough hillside past several small lochans. The going is very slow here and the path is sometimes difficult to follow. Reach a point after about 3km, just short of some crags, where easy slopes lead down to the left to cross the Abhainn an Loch Bhig. This same point can be reached by the Falls option by either ascending directly to reach the main path, or by a slow, rising traverse.

Once across the stream, a short, steep ascent leads to a relatively flat area dominated by a sizeable hill loch, (Loch nan Caorach), beyond which stands the Stack of Glencoul. Follow the west side of the loch, on tussocky pathless terrain, and cross a stream at its northern end. Climb the final steep slopes to reach the airy little summit.

The finest view is north-west, along the blue expanse of Loch Glencoul, which is enclosed by steep glaciated slopes. There is also a superb view of the Falls, a long ribbon of white across the glen.

Return by the outward route.

81. FARRMHEALL (521M/1,709FT)

MAP	OS SHEET 9 (GR 308588)
DISTANCE	4KM
ASCENT	340M
TIME	1.5–2 HRS
ACCESS	A838 (GR 310570)
DIFFICULTY	EASY, GRASSY BUT PATHLESS ASCENT
SUMMARY	Farrmheall is the highest point of the wild and distinctly hilly tract of land lying south of Cape Wrath and north of the Rhiconich to Durness road. One of four Hughs in this unfrequented region, it is the easiest to access.

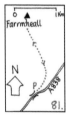

THE FOUR MAIN hills in the remote region south of Cape Wrath all have great character, but their inaccessibility (apart from Farrmheall) has ensured that the only visitors they receive are hardened hillwalking connoisseurs. Farrmheall is a fine introduction to the area and gives terrific views from its summit.

The derivation of the name 'Farrmheall' is possibly from the Gaelic '*farrad mheall*', meaning 'near hill'. It is certainly near the A838 and can easily be climbed as a short leg-stretcher while en route north or south.

There is a small parking area just beyond the bridge on the north side of the road, about 5 miles north of Rhiconich. From here, make your way up the broad southern spur of the hill, heading for an obvious rocky outcrop.

Initially, the going is over tussocks and boggy ground, but higher up, beyond the outcrop, the angle eases and a vague all terrain vehicle track takes the line of least resistance.

The summit area is very flat and covered with grey quartzite blocks, but there is a fair-sized cairn surrounded by a grassy mantle. Northwards, the peaks of Fashven and Creag Riabhach are in view, while to the north-east the white beaches of the Faraid Head peninsula should be visible. To the south, the Corbetts of Fionaven and Cranstackie dominate the landscape.

Return by the route of ascent.

Summit of Farmheall

82. AN GRIANAN THE SUNNY SPOT (467M/1,532FT)
83. CREAG RIABHACH BRINDLED ROCKY PEAK (485M/1,592FT)

MAP	OS SHEET 9 (GR 264627, 279638)
DISTANCE	24KM
ASCENT	750M
TIME	7–9 HRS
ACCESS	TRACK JUNCTION AT OLDSHORE BEG (GR 205596)
DIFFICULTY	LONG, PARTLY BOGGY APPROACH PATH, THEN WILD, CRAGGY AND PATHLESS TERRAIN
SUMMARY	In the heart of the rolling tract of wilderness south of Cape Wrath, these are among the wildest peaks in Scotland and certainly two of the remotest described in this book.

A VARIETY OF possible scenarios present themselves in tackling these two fine hills, including an overnight stay in Strathan Bothy, or a long circular route, with a visit to legendary Sandwood Bay. They could also be combined with Fashven, to the north-east, on a backpack across the region. However, the described route, while the most direct, involves much ascent and descent.

About a mile before the parking area for Sandwood Bay, a track goes off to the right, past a wooden house. There is space to park just up the road from here. Follow the track across heathery moorland for about 1km and look out for several cairns marking the start of a path forking off to the right in an easterly direction.

Take this path, which leads in 1km to the first, and largest, of two lochans, Loch Mor a'Chraisg (Loch of the Big Crossing), where the path becomes patchy, but is partly marked by a few posts. The route follows the northern shore of the loch and continues to a smaller lochan, also following the north shore.

Shortly after this, the path descends into the green and sheltered Strath Shinary, a pleasant change from lonely moor. The river here flows into Sandwood Loch, whose outflow is Sandwood Bay. The path makes a sharp turn left near the river and crosses it by a suspension bridge. After crossing the river, head up

towards Strathan Bothy, a stone cottage about 300m away in a sheltered position below the hill behind. Like many Highland cottages, Strathan was once permanently occupied by crofters who scraped a living from the surrounding land. It is now one of many bothies maintained (but not owned) by the Mountain Bothies Association for use as a shelter and overnight stay by weary backpackers – and of course for day-trippers en route to two wild hills.

Ascend easy, grassy slopes behind the bothy and cross a depression to gain steeper ground leading up to Sron a'Ghobhair (nose of the goat) the southern shoulder of An Grianan. Ascend the steep little nose, bypassing any crags, to reach a flat, grassy area

with An Grianan prominent ahead.

A broad ridge on the left winds round clockwise over a small hillock, onto the airy summit of An Grianan in less than 2km. The summit cairn is perched right on the edge of a craggy sandstone cliff, unmarked on the Landranger map, and there is a marvellous view across Loch a'Phuill Bhuidh (possibly 'loch of the yellow round stone') to the second hill of Creag Riabhach.

To avoid descending the cliff, retrace your steps west for a few hundred metres, before dropping down easy slopes to the sandy eastern shore of the loch, where there is a fine view looking back to the cone of An Grianan, topped by its rocky crown.

Ascend Creag Riabhach by its

An Grianan from Loch a' Phuill Bhuidhe

An Grianan from Creag Riabhach

Fashven from Creag Riabhach

south-western spur, on layered sandstone terraces, to the summit trig point. The finest feature of this hill is its steep north-easterly scarp slope, stretching for 1.5km, the edge of which is followed on the return route. The summit of this hill is a lonely outpost indeed and gives a true flavour of this remote region.

Leave the summit and follow the edge of the scarp slope in a south-easterly direction, enjoying a glorious bird's-eye view of the surrounding landscape. In less than 1km turn right to head south-westwards down gentle slopes to the flat area south-east of the lochan. Ascend slightly past a tiny lochan before descending the north side of the Allt na Rainich (Burn of the Fern). At the point where the burn begins to drop away down steeper slopes, traverse off to the right along a deer track for about 0.5km, before descending easier ground to the vicinity of the bothy. From here, follow the outward route back to the start.

84. FASHVEN FAS-BHEINN – UNCULTIVATED (WILD) HILL (460M/1,508FT)

MAP	OS SHEET 9 (GR 313674)
DISTANCE	12KM
ASCENT	550M
TIME	3.5–5 HRS
ACCESS	CAPE WRATH ROAD (GR 327693)
DIFFICULTY	WILD, PATHLESS TERRAIN WITH A STEEP ASCENT
SUMMARY	Almost at Cape Wrath, Fashven is the most northerly hill in this book. Unique wilderness character and sublime sea views make its ascent worth the effort.

THE ONLY PRACTICABLE method of ascending this hill is to make use of the passenger ferry service across the Kyle of Durness, which connects with a minibus taking visitors to Cape Wrath. Just ask the driver to drop you off at the bend in the road, south of Loch Inshore, which is the closest point to the hill. The route includes Fashven and also Ben Akie (another Marilyn), finishing at the road-end ferry slipway. The ferry runs between May and September and usually starts around

9.30 AM, though it may be cancelled, depending on weather, tidal conditions, MOD exercises and passenger uptake. Contact the ferry operator, J Morrison, for details (Tel: 01971 511246).

On the rattly minibus drive to Cape Wrath, the steep-sided Fashven is very prominent to the west, rising up out of the featureless moor. From the drop-off point near Loch Inshore, strike off south, across tussocks and bog, heading for an incongruous object of shocking pink. On closer inspection, the object turns out to be an old armoured vehicle, apparently painted by schoolchildren in order that it stands out for use in bombing practice. Much of this area is used by the MOD for training purposes and at one point Cape Wrath was in danger of being permanently out of bounds – thankfully

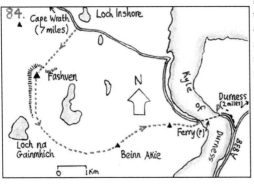

Fashven from Creag Riabhach

this failed to materialise. I just hope it will be exempt from any gung-ho windfarm developers.

Ascend the obvious right-hand spur of Fashven on a rapidly steepening slope, avoiding a band of sandstone crags by traversing off to the right. Reach a sandstone terrace marking the summit area, where there is a small and a large cairn together with a small radio mast. Enjoy the fine views, especially over the Kyle of Durness to Faraid Head and beyond.

Descend the long and easy-angled south ridge on slabs and scree to Loch na Gainmich, before

gradually swinging south-east down grassy slopes to reach the boggy col separating Fashven from Beinn Akie. Ascend Beinn Akie on easy, grassy slopes to reach its craggy summit, with a fine view looking back to Fashven.

A direct route to the ferry point can be made from here by heading to the subsidiary top of Beinn an Amair and then dropping down its north-eastern spur. Alternatively, omit this top and descend easier slopes to reach the road about 1km up from the ferry point.

Summit of Fashven

85. MEALL MEADHONACH MIDDLE HILL (422M/1,385FT)
86. BEINN CEANNABEINNE HILL OF THE HEADLAND (383M/1,257FT)

MAP	OS SHEET 9 (GR 410628, 423647)
DISTANCE	11KM
ASCENT	500M
TIME	3.5–5 HRS
ACCESS	DURNESS, LOCH MEADAIDH TRACK (GR 412668)
DIFFICULTY	GOOD APPROACH TRACK THEN RUGGED PATHLESS TERRAIN
SUMMARY	Beinn Ceannabeinne's craggy western profile is a striking feature from the coastal village of Durness and its south-western higher twin of Meall Meadhonach combine to make a tasty twosome of rocky peaks – ideal for a summer's evening.

ACCESS TO THESE two hills is particularly easy, due to some recently upgraded tracks and paths starting form the A838 main road in Durness. Drive south along the partly tarmac minor road, beginning just to the east of the big A838 loop near Sango Bay. There are several parking spaces on the right after the last house.

Walk south from here through a gate and onto a rough vehicle track leading to Loch Meadaidh. A few hundred metres before the loch, turn left along the path, crossing the stream by some massive stepping-stones. This stalkers' track ascends gradually over heather moor to the wide col between the two peaks. You will pass the junction of another track going off

to the left which reaches the main road 1km further east than the approach track. This could also be used as an alternative approach route.

The described route ascends Meall Meadhonach first, though you may prefer to climb the other peak first. Near the end of the track, break off to the right and head west to a small lochan hidden in a dip between the main summit and a small subsidiary top. From here, climb craggy slopes to the fairly extensive summit plateau and the prominent cairn balanced on a shattered bastion of rocky outcrops.

The views are magnificent, especially northwards to Faraid Head and the coastline. The peak of An Lean-

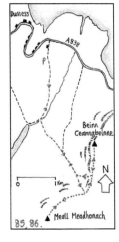

Beinn Ceannabeinne

Charn is very prominent across Loch Eriboll to the south (another Hugh).

Return to the col and ascend gentle, grassy slopes north to reach the summit trig point of Beinn Ceannabeinne, perched on a large slab of Lewisian Gneiss. This is a grand spot to linger on a fine summer's evening.

There are a variety of possible descent routes back to the starting point, all roughly the same distance. The recommended route returns by the route of ascent for about 0.5km, before dropping down to reach the path by a grassy depression between the crags.

It is possible to descend west, down initially steep slopes, and pick up the second track mentioned in the ascent description. However, there are numerous steep crags around the summit and route-finding may be a problem.

Thirdly, a longer outing can be made by descending north-east on easy grassy slopes above the craggy western flank. This leads to the main road in 1.5km, where you turn left and follow it back to the start.

Beinn Ceannabeinne from Meall Meadhonach

87. AN LEAN-CHARN CONNECTING CAIRN, POSSIBLY (521M/1,709FT)

MAP	OS SHEET 9 (GR 420526)
DISTANCE	8KM
ASCENT	520M
TIME	2.5–4 HRS
ACCESS	HEAD OF LOCH ERIBOLL (GR 394538)
DIFFICULTY	MAINLY WILD, RUGGED, PATHLESS TERRAIN
SUMMARY	This hill's distinctive, flat-topped, wedge-like appearance is very obvious on the drive south along the western side of Loch Eriboll. Though not far from a main road, it possesses a wonderfully wild and rocky character.

AN LEAN-CHARN LIES right on the edge of the so-called Moine Thrust fault line, a 160km geological line running between the Sleat peninsula on Skye and Loch Eriboll. Below this line is the huge mass of Moine Schists, while above it lie the gneiss, Torridonian sandstone and Cambrian quartzite-limestone of which An Lean-Charn is composed.

Begin at the start of the rough vehicle track which heads south to Strabeg and leaves the A838 single-track road at the southern end of Loch Eriboll. Note that parking here is very limited and you should not block the entrance to the track.

Walk south along the track under the imposing crags of Creag na Faoilinn (Crag of the Sea-Gull) for about 1km, then turn left to ascend tussocky, but easy-angled slopes, crossing a fence higher up. After ascending some 200m of height, reach a flat, grassy area containing three

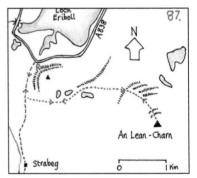

lochans, forming the complex col between Creag na Faoilinn and An Lean-Charn.

From here, head east across undulating terrain to reach the significantly steeper western flank of An Lean-Charn.

As you climb higher, you will notice the unusual rock outcrops of quartzite-limestone, forming horizontal stepped bedding planes, some of which offer excellent scrambling opportunities. You will pass a couple of small lochans

An Lean-Charn from Loch Eriboll

before reaching the final summit crags, a castle-like promontory with a small summit cairn.

The panorama is truly magnificent, with Ben Hope (the most northerly Munro) stealing the skyline to the south-east, while the rock and scree buttresses of Foinaven dominate the western prospect. To the south is a wilderness of rock and heather with

View from An Lean-Charn

An Lean-Charn from the South

a sprinkling of minor lochans and smaller summits. The view north is dominated by the long sea-arm of Loch Eriboll.

The time and distance information is given based on a return by the route of ascent but for those wishing a longer day it is a good idea to continue southwards along a broad rocky ridge before descending west to the vicinity of Strabeg and following the path northwards to the start.

88. BEN HUTIG (408M/1,338FT)

MAP	OS SHEET 10 (GR 538653)
DISTANCE	10KM
ASCENT	400M
TIME	3–4 HRS
ACCESS	ACHININVER (GR 568647)
DIFFICULTY	EASY APPROACH TRACK AND GENTLE, GRASSY SLOPES
SUMMARY	This fine, wee hill stands in splendid isolation right at the head of the wild and windswept peninsula of A'Mhoine (Peat Moor) between Loch Eriboll and the Kyle of Tongue. It is seen to advantage from the A838 road which crosses the barren crest of this lonely moor.

THE NAME HUTIG is most likely derived from the Norse '*hvitir*', meaning 'white headland', pertaining to the exposed rocky headland of Whiten Head to the north-west. Like An Lean-Charn, it stands on the edge of the Moine Thrust fault line and its summit crags are partly Cambrian quartzite and limestone. It may not possess the striking profile of other hills in this book but its sublime summit views give a unique appreciation of this peerless, lonely landscape.

A fine circular route begins at the lonely hamlet of Achininver which can be reached by a 6-mile drive from the A838 at a point west of the Kyle of Tongue just before the bridge/causeway. It is signposted as Melness. Park just beyond the bridge over the Strath Melness Burn, from where a vehicle track heads directly uphill past farm buildings.

Walk up this track, as it meanders

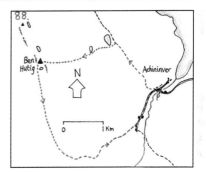

upwards through common grazing land and, in about 1.5km, to Loch na h-Uamnachd. Leave the track here and head off left (wsw) across open moorland directly towards the summit crags of Ben Hutig, less than 2km away. The going is relatively easy, on firm but sometimes tussocky terrain, and you will pass a smaller lochan en route.

Ben Hutig's long summit ridge contains three tops, the middle one being the highest point, crowned with

Ben Hutig

a trig point. The summit area is very unusual, as it possesses a collection of curious stone-built shelters with proper entrances, the trig point enclosed by one. These were possibly wartime lookout shelters. The most northerly top 1km away has a very prominent cairn.

The sheer sense of space and remoteness from anywhere is vividly apparent from this lonely outpost. The striking profiles of Ben Loyal and Ben Hope rising from the surrounding moorland is perhaps the most arresting sight.

After lunching and a prolonged fester on this marvellous spot, begin the descent southwards past the southern top and a small lochan to eventually rendezvous with a vehicle track about 2.5km from the summit at GR 548633. Follow this to the minor road at West Strathan where you follow it northwards for 1km to your point of departure. This completes a very satisfying round trip.

Summit of Ben Hutig

89. MEALLAN LIATH SMALL GREY LUMP (601M/1,972FT)

MAP	OS SHEETS 9/10 (GR 514503)
DISTANCE	12KM
ASCENT	660M
TIME	4–6 HRS
ACCESS	HEAD OF KYLE OF TONGUE (GR 554527)
DIFFICULTY	EASY APPROACH TRACK THEN VERY RUGGED TERRAIN WITH SEVERAL STEEP SECTIONS
SUMMARY	Meallan Liath's unnamed north-eastern outlier stands out as a rocky conical peak with a wonderfully craggy ridge leading to Meallan Liath itself. The hill occupies a fine location between Ben Hope and Ben Loyal, giving glorious views of both.

THE ENGLISH TRANSLATION of this hill's name severely understates the charm and appeal of what is a rocky, complex peak with great character. Its craggy north face and north-east ridge of folded Moine Schists is its greatest feature.

The obvious route to this hill would be via the track passing Kinloch Lodge and Cottage, but despite the Land Reform Act of 2003, the owners have seen fit to erect a sign indicating no public access by this route. However, a suitable alternative is available by driving north for several hundred metres until you are able to park at a grassy area below a large unoccupied house on the west side of the minor road.

Walk up the track to the left of the house and then turn left along a continuation (unmarked on earlier maps). Reach a junction after a few hundred metres. To the right is the

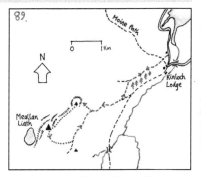

ancient Moine Path to Loch Hope, while the left branch goes to Kinloch Lodge. Continue ahead through gorse bushes on a good vehicle track, as it rises gradually onto a wide, heathery ridge. From here, there is a fine view of the craggy, conical outlier of Meallan Liath, your first main objective. The multi-summited Ben Loyal is also well seen from here. The prominent little rocky cone of Sgor Fhionnaich on the right was considered a worthy 'Hugh'

On the ridge of Meallan Liath

contender, but is really a part of the Ben Loyal group of tops.

Descend gradually, before turning off left on another track which slowly ascends to join a secondary track from the main Kinloch track. Turn right and follow this track as it degenerates into an all terrain vehicle stalkers' track which bypasses the Meallan Liath ridge on the eastern flank.

Leave this track to ascend the steep, craggy north-eastern spur, where there are small pockets of scrambling if the rock is dry. The summit area of this outlying peak is composed of huge fins of folded schist rock and care should be taken on the descent southwards to the continuation ridge.

After about 0.5km, reach an impasse on the ridge, in the form of a 20m-high slabby wall. This can be circumvented by moving round to the left to reach a recess, where a rock step on the left gives access to a long, easy-angled grassy ramp which should be followed to the top. Here, move left and soon reach a second 'bad step', which can be climbed by a steep grass gully or again, by moving round to easier ground on the left.

Complex rocky terrain leads to the final col below Meallan Liath, which is easily reached by gentle, grassy slopes and minor crags.

A reasonable sized cairn on a slab is not the highest point, which is about 100m to the south-west. The summit area, a chaotic mass of slabs, crags and perched boulders (erratics), offers stunning views of both Ben Loyal and the remote eastern corries of Ben Hope with their massive lochans.

Adventurous and energetic souls could easily continue westwards

Summit of Meallan Liath

and ascend Ben Hope by any one of several east-facing spurs. For those with more modest ambitions, descend south-eastwards from the summit on gentle slopes and broad slabs to eventually rejoin the track in the defile between Meallan Liath and Carn a Mhadaidh, another prominent, outlying peak, with some striking outcrops on its northern flank.

Follow the stalkers' track easily along the steep south-eastern flank of the Meallan Liath ridge to rejoin the route of ascent.

Ben Loyal from Meallan Liath

90. CNOC AN FHREICEADAIN WATCH HILL (307M/1,007FT)

MAP	OS SHEET 10 (GR 611594)
DISTANCE	3KM
ASCENT	250M
TIME	1–2 HRS
ACCESS	COLDBACKIE (GR 613600)
DIFFICULTY	INTERMITTENT PATH AND STEEP HEATHERY ASCENT
SUMMARY	This distinctive, heathery knoll towers proudly over the Kyle of Tongue and is well seen on the drive east across the causeway. It is a phenomenal viewpoint, well worth the short, steep ascent.

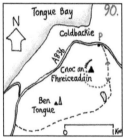

THE NAME 'WATCH HILL' suggests that this hill was used as a lookout post in times gone by, and indeed, its strategic position high about Tongue Bay would be an asset not overlooked by Vikings or Bronze Age people.

Oddly enough, there is no proper path to the top. However, a useful path begins at Coldbackie to the north of the hill and traverses round its flank (and that of Ben Tongue, the slightly lower hill to the south-west supporting a radio mast).

Begin at Coldbackie on the A836, where there is limited parking on the seaward side of the road. A signpost indicates the start of the path at a wooden gate near a house. Follow the path for about 1km, as it winds its way round the steep, heathery east flank of the hill. Leave the path before the small lochan (An Dubh-loch) and head up a grassy depression leading to the broad col between Ben Tongue and Cnoc an Fhreiceadain.

A path of sorts doubles back up the southern slopes of the hill to gain the flat top surmounted by a trig point.

The seaward view is magnificent over Tongue Bay and the Rabbit Islands, while the multi-topped fortress of Ben Loyal dominates the scene to the south.

For a longer excursion, continue south-west for 1km to Ben Tongue, but the view from here is not any better and the radio mast detracts from the scene. Note that the north-eastern flank of the hill has a line of sheer crags and a descent down this side is not recommended. Return by the route of ascent.

Summit of Cnoc an Fhreiceadain

91. BEN HIEL (535M/1,754FT)

MAP	OS SHEET 10 (GR 596501)
DISTANCE	5KM
ASCENT	420M
TIME	2–3 HRS
ACCESS	A836 ROAD – NORTH OF LOCH LOYAL (GR 615506)
DIFFICULTY	TUSSOCKY AND PATHLESS ASCENT
summary	Ben Hiel is the closest of Ben Loyal's satellite summits but is still far enough and distinctive enough to be considered a separate hill in its own right – unlike Point 568 on the western side of Ben Loyal.

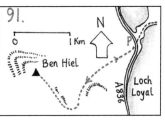

THE NAME 'HIEL' is almost certainly of Norse origin and possibly derived from 'ha fjall', meaning 'high fell'. It would be perfectly feasible to include the hill with an ascent of Ben Loyal but most people will probably opt to climb it on a separate occasion.

The quickest ascent is from the A836 road to the east and uses the same lay-by as for Beinn Stumanadh. (Route 93). Head up open hillside in the general direction of a radio mast. The going is quite tiring, through bracken and tussocky grass. Reach a more level section and make for the col and the base of the hill's south-east ridge. Once on the ridge, reach drier terrain and craggy outcrops with several humps and bumps, before reaching the small cairn marking the summit.

The top gives a fine view of Ben Loyal itself and of the conical outline of Cnoc nan Cuilean to the south, Ben Loyal's highest satellite top. Return by the route of ascent.

Ben Hiel from Cnoc nan Cuilean

92. CNOC NAN CUILEAN KNOLL OF THE CUB OR PUP (557M/1,828FT)

MAP	OS SHEET 10 (GR 597462)
DISTANCE	4KM
ASCENT	450M
TIME	2–3 HRS
ACCESS	A836 – MILESTONE LAY-BY (GR 613449)
DIFFICULTY	FAIRLY STEEP, GRASSY, PATHLESS ASCENT
SUMMARY	This is probably the most prominent, and the highest, of Ben Loyal's attendant peaks and gives glorious views from its airy summit.

CNOC NAN CUILEAN'S craggy and conical profile is seen to advantage during the drive south along the west side of Loch Loyal and gives the impression of a much higher hill. There is a fine view of the hill from the old cottage at Lettermore and this would be a good starting point for those wishing to complete a circular traverse of the peak.

The described route, however, begins at the large, grassy lay-by some 2 miles to the south, although any point along this road down to the bridge at Inchkinloch would be a suitable starting point.

Ascend easy, grassy slopes that gradually steepen as height is gained, eventually reaching the peaty col

Cnoc nan Cuilean

View East from Cnoc nan Cuilean

between Meall Eudainn and the short southern spur of the main hill. There is a fine view of Ben Hiel through this gap with a pair of lochans making a suitable foreground.

Head directly for the hill's southern spur across tussocky terrain, until a final steepening on shorter grass, crowberry and minor outcrops brings you to the flat, grassy summit, topped by a small cairn.

The sheer sense of space of the Flow country to the south and east is very pronounced on this grand wee summit and the twin cones of Ben Griam Mor and Ben Griam Beag stand proud on the horizon beyond vast peatlands peppered with lochans.

Descend by the route of ascent.

93. BEINN STUMANADH (527M/1,728FT)

MAP	OS SHEET 10 (GR 641499)
DISTANCE	8KM
ASCENT	410M
TIME	2–3.5 HRS
ACCESS	A836 ROAD – NORTH OF LOCH LOYAL (GR 615506)
DIFFICULTY	GENTLE, GRASSY, BUT PATHLESS TERRAIN
SUMMARY	Beinn Stumanadh stands in splendid isolation on the east side of Loch Loyal and to the east of Ben Loyal. Its northern horseshoe ridge makes a fine expedition.

BEINN STUMANADH'S ORIGIN is most likely '*beinn sturr manadh*' or 'rugged hill of the apparition'; 'modest hill' is another possibility. Of the three wee hills in Ben Loyal's eastern shadow, this is probably the best, and a loyal subject to the Queen of Scottish mountains.

The obvious starting point is at a small lay-by on the A836 Tongue to Lairg road, between Loch Loyal and Loch Craggie. Here, a path crosses the small causeway between the two lochs to reach the steep northern slopes of the hill.

Follow this path over a wooden bridge crossing the connecting river between the lochs and onto the gravelly shoreline at the north end of Loch Loyal. Reach the other side of the loch and follow the path as it passes below a wooded area on the steep northern slopes of Sron Ruadh (Red Nose), the end point of the north-western spur of Beinn Stumanadh.

It is possible to climb directly up to Sron Ruadh from any point on this path, but easier to continue to the old building of Achnanclach before turning south then west to reach the flat, grassy top of Sron Ruadh. From here, follow the obvious grassy ridge south-east, gradually swinging round left on steeper slopes to reach the summit trig point of Beinn Stumanadh.

The finest view is looking over Loch Loyal to Ben Loyal, while to the south Ben Kilbreck is very obvious. The twin summits of Ben Griam Mor and Ben Griam Beg are both prominent landmarks to the south-east, standing

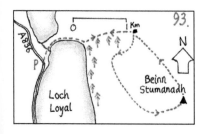

Beinn Stumanadh

proud in an otherwise boggy, watery wilderness.

Descend the northern spur of the hill on initially easy-angled slopes, before steeper slopes take you down to the vicinity of Achnanclach. Cross the burn and rejoin the path used on the ascent to take you back to the starting point.

94. BEN GRIAM MOR BIG DARK HILL (590M/1,936FT)
95. BEN GRIAM BEG LITTLE DARK HILL (580M/1,902FT)

MAP	OS SHEET 10 AND 17 (GR 806389, 832412)
DISTANCE	15KM
ASCENT	800M
TIME	4.5–6 HRS
ACCESS	B871, SOUTH-EAST OF GARVAULT HOTEL (GR 787379)
DIFFICULTY	MAINLY TUSSOCKY GROUND WITH SOME BOG, INTERMITTENT PATH
SUMMARY	The twin cones of 'the Griams' thrusting proudly out of the surrounding Flow country are distinctive landmarks for miles around. Their ascent gives a fine circuit and a real appreciation of the expansive, wild quality of this unique region.

THE FLOW COUNTRY of Caithness and Sutherland is a vast tract of desolate peatland covering some 3,900 square miles, stretching from Loch Loyal in the west to the ragged, cliff-girt coastline of Caithness. Formed around 7,000 years ago, when an all-pervasive plant called sphagnum moss began to thrive in the water-logged, oxygen-starved conditions caused by a wetter climate, the area has remained largely untouched by the hand of man – until the late 20th century. It was then that the profit-driven motives of mankind saw the development of quick-growing, tax-deductible blanket forestry and latterly the spread of monstrous, inefficient monuments to climate change – namely, wind-

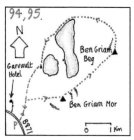

turbines.

While some may see the Flow country as a barren landscape, ripe for such development, the truth is that the area is a precious heritage with an ecological importance that cannot be understated. A wildlife wonderland, rich in plant, bird and animal life, the Flow country has been described by international conservationists as having unique global importance as the largest area of blanket bog in Europe. It is one of the world's outstanding ecosystems, comparable with Brazil's equatorial rainforest and Africa's Serengeti.

From a cartographical point of view, the Griams are awkwardly placed, each being on the edge of two separate Landranger maps. Though

Ben Griam Beg from Ben Griam Mor

the hills can be approached from the east via the track to Greamachary, the most satisfying round begins on the western side, just south of the Garvault Hotel. Park near the start of an anglers' path which heads into Loch Coire nam Mang.

Follow this path for 1km before striking off eastwards up grass and heather slopes to reach the north-west spur of Ben Griam Mor. The ridge soon steepens considerably, with some rocky outcrops before you reach the flat summit area and cairn.

Enjoy the extensive summit panorama of majestic moor and loch before descending the well-defined north-east ridge of Ben Griam Mor, heading directly for Ben Griam Beg. The intervening col is usually nothing other than a boggy morass, but by judicious route-finding it is possible to retain dry feet.

Now on OS map 10, ascend Ben Griam Beg by its vague south-west ridge, traversing a level shoulder just below the final pull to the summit. Bronze Age folk were quick to realise the hill's potential for security and built a fort on the summit, securing an uninterrupted outlook in all directions. The remains of thick stone walls and enclosures cover a large area around the summit and the hill hosts the highest hill fort of its kind in the country.

The highest point of the hill has a trig point just east of the fort remnants. From here, descend north-west, keeping north of a line of

Ben Griam Beg from Loch Coire nam Mang

crags lower down the hill and head for the north end of Loch Druim a'Chliabhain (possibly meaning 'loch by the ridge of creels'). Stay on higher ground to avoid the worst of the bog. In the vicinity of the loch, the ground becomes drier and a vague path follows the north shore.

Take time to savour the peace and tranquillity of the surroundings. If you are lucky, you may hear the haunting cry of a red-throated diver, or the plaintive piping of greenshank and plovers. The cry of the curlew will also resonate with the sight of sparkling blue lochs and sweeping moors.

On reaching the western extremity of Loch Druim a'Chliabhain, leave the loch entirely to avoid a boggy area and keep to higher ground on the west, heading south to the red-roofed boathouse on the west shore of the smaller Loch Coire nam Mang (meaning 'loch of the corrie of the fawn').

From the boathouse, join the path taking you round the northern slopes of Ben Griam Mor to your starting point.

96. MAIDEN PAP MAIDEN'S BREAST (484M/1,587FT)

MAP	OS SHEET 17 (GR 048293)
DISTANCE	6KM
ASCENT	320M
TIME	2–3 HRS
ACCESS	BRAEMORE PUBLIC ROAD END (GR 073305)
DIFFICULTY	GOOD APPROACH TRACK THEN A FAIRLY STEEP BUT GRASSY ASCENT; OPTIONAL SCRAMBLING
SUMMARY	The splendid rocky cone of Maiden Pap is arguably shapelier than its more popular 'Graham' neighbour of Morven, further west. It forms a worthwhile objective in its own right, or could be included as part of a bigger round.

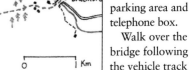

TUCKED AWAY IN the wild south-east corner of Caithness are clustered a curious mixture of steep-sided little hills, including Morven, Smean, Scaraben and Maiden Pap. The latter is by fair the rockiest, and certainly the lowest of the four, and despite being often dismissed as a miniature version of Morven, I would class it as having greater character

To reach Braemore, leave the A9 Brora to Wick road just south of Dunbeath and follow the minor road for 7 miles to the end of the public road, where there is a small parking area and telephone box.

Walk over the bridge following the vehicle track as it passes several farm cottages and through a metal gate beyond. Maiden Pap is very prominent ahead and to the left of the track. Go through a second gate into an area of Scots Pine forest and emerge a few hundred metres later onto open moorland.

The track continues slightly uphill to follow a line of trees on the right. At the point where trees appear on the left, turn off the track

Maiden Pap

Morven from Maiden Pap

to the left to follow the edge of the plantation on a faint, boggy path.

The steep slopes of Maiden Pap are now directly ahead but appear to offer no definitive line of ascent other than a heathery runnel between crags. This feature rises directly up the north side of the hill, separating a small subsidiary top from the main summit.

On leaving the plantation, head directly for this runnel and ascend it on a vague path. If you are allergic to steep ascents, there is a less steep route on the south side of the hill, which is the continuation of this depression on the opposite side and forms the descent route.

Reach a level area between the twin tops and turn right to climb a steep, grassy path which soon emerges on the flat, airy summit, devoid of a cairn.

There is a fine view of Morven (Big Hill) a few kilometres to the west and also of Smean with its curious rocky tors. The gaunt wilderness to the north is utterly devoid of any notable features other than the gentle contours of remote Ben Alisky.

For a less steep descent, return to the level area and descend right on easy slopes between outcrops of rough sandstone conglomerate peppering the southern slopes of the hill. Some of these outcrops provide pockets of scrambling, but are too broken to provide any lengthy, worthwhile routes.

Gradually veer left below the crags to contour round the eastern flank of the hill and return to the forest edge to rejoin the ascent route.

97. CREAG SCALABSDALE (555M/1,820FT)

MAP	OS SHEET 17 (GR 970241)
DISTANCE	19KM
ASCENT	700M
TIME	6–8 HRS
ACCESS	SUISGILL LODGE, A897 (GR 901237)
DIFFICULTY	GOOD APPROACH AND RETURN TRACKS, CENTRAL SECTION TUSSOCKY AND PATHLESS
SUMMARY	This wonderfully remote little hill has great presence and character and its ascent gives a fine appreciation of the wild, rolling hill country east of the Strath of Kildonan.

A GLANCE AT the upper right half of OS map 17 shows a handful of hill set apart from the rest by the closeness of their contours. These include Morven and Scaraben (Grahams); and Maiden Pap and Creag Scalabsdale (Marilyns and Hughs).

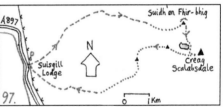

The origin of the name Scalabsdale is likely to be Norse, the clue being the name 'Skelabosdale', a broad ridge south of the hill named as such on the OS map. The letter 'k' does not feature in the Gaelic language and 'skalli' in Norse is 'bald-headed'. However, 'sgailc' is Gaelic for baldness, so perhaps the name is a fusion of both languages. Certainly, the summit and long, narrow north-east ridge has a bald and featureless appearance.

The starting point for the ascent is the Strath of Kildonan, a wide and fertile glen which bore particularly bad witness to the Highland Clearances, three quarters of the area's crofters being forcefully evicted from their homes to make way for sheep.

Park at Suisgill Lodge, in a wooded area about a mile south of the bridge over the Suisgill Burn at Upper Suisgill. From here, follow a track directly up the hill to meet another track in a few hundred metres. Turn left along this well-made stalkers' track, as it gradually ascends the north-western flanks of Cnoc a'Mheadhoinn to cross its level northern spur, before descending into a grassy hollow. The track has now deteriorated into a grassy furrow, but its line is still obvious on the gradual

The author on Creag Scalabsdale (photo: Ken Black)

ascent up a broad spur leading to Creag Scalabsdale.

The sense of complete isolation begins to take over as you finally reach the end of the track, 6km from the road. Make for the conspicuous little knoll of Suidh' an Fhir-bhig, helpfully translated on the map as 'The Child's Seat', a curious little craggy peaklet which begs to be climbed.

From here, cross the wide, tussocky bowl containing Loch Scalabsdale to reach Creag Scalabsdale's wide western ridge and follow it upwards to the grassy summit, which is topped with a sizeable cairn of quartzite blocks. Enjoy a fine view of Morven, Maiden Pap and Scaraben to the north-east while savouring the delicious desolation of this far-flung hill.

A fine circular tour can be accomplished by following the ascent ridge down to the wide col above the loch and then climbing Creag nan Gearr (Rock of the Hare), before continuing west to another col and ascending Cnoc Salislade (origin uncertain). This is now within striking distance of another stalkers' track leading back to the start.

Drop south from Cnoc Salislade, before turning south-west down steeper slopes to a wide col. Go over another small top and descend this in a south-westerly direction to reach a stream, and the start of the path. The start of the path may be tricky to find, but once found it is easy to follow. It descends to cross the Kildonan Burn, before the final 2km back to Suisgill Lodge.

98. BEN HORN HILL OF THE EAGLE (521M/1,710FT)

MAP	OS SHEET 17 (GR 807064)
DISTANCE	4KM
ASCENT	300M
TIME	1.5–2.5 HRS
ACCESS	BRIDGE OF HORN (GR 800047)
DIFFICULTY	FOREST TRACK THEN GENTLE TUSSOCKY, PATHLESS ASCENT
SUMMARY	The bald top of Ben Horn sits in splendid isolation above Loch Horn and Dunrobin Glen and is a marvellous viewpoint.

BEN HORN'S MOST distinctive feature is its rocky eastern prow, which is well appreciated from Beinn a'Bhragaidh above Golspie, 5km to the south (see Route 99). The described route from Bridge of Horn in Dunrobin Glen is the quickest route and misses this feature. However, a short detour with some loss of height could be considered in order to check out this possible

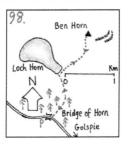

sporting ascent.

On a recent second ascent of this hill I was rather disappointed to discover that a new windfarm had suddenly sprung up to the north and west of the summit and this has detracted from its wild quality.

Drive up through the scattered settlement of Backies above Golspie and park just beyond the Bridge of Horn. You will no doubt see signs

Ben Horn from Beinn a'Bhragaidh

Ben Horn from Loch Horn

indicating Kilbraur Windfarm. There is also much recent forestry to the north of the road.

Walk up the forest track, gaining height quickly, until it swings left heading for a large metal gate at the forest edge. Cross the deer fence by a wooden stepped stile to the left and reach Loch Horn (actually a reservoir) in a few hundred metres.

Ben Horn rises to the north-east of the loch in gentle heather and tussocky slopes. If you wish to view or ascend the steep eastern prow, you will need to drop east from the low bealach between Loch Horn and its undistinguished southern top. As you ascend the hill, several turbines will appear to the east and north, but the views from the small summit cairn are still worth the effort. The 'Ben Bhraggie' monument to the south is very prominent (see Route 99). Return by the route of ascent.

99. BEINN A'BHRAGAIDH BRACKISH HILL, POSSIBLY (394M/1,293FT)

MAP	OS SHEET 17 (GR 815009)
DISTANCE	8KM
ASCENT	390M
TIME	2–3 HRS
ACCESS	GOLSPIE–FOUNTAIN ROAD CAR PARK (GR 833000)
DIFFICULTY	GOOD PATHS AND TRACKS THROUGHOUT
SUMMARY	This hill occupies a commanding position above the coastal town of Golspie and is immediately recognised by its enormous summit monument to the First Duke of Sutherland. It is a phenomenal viewpoint worth every inch of the ascent.

BEINN A'BHRAIGAIDH IS known locally as Ben Bhraggie and the name possibly derives from '*breac*' or '*bhreac*', meaning 'speckled' or 'brackish', although it may also commemorate Saint Brachdaidh.

The hill is held in fond regard by Golspie residents, though the monument at the top has provoked the passions of folk knowledgeable about the Clearances – more on this later.

In the centre of Golspie, at the car park at the junction of Fountain Road with the A9, there is an information board with an outline of the route up the hill and a potted history of the Duke and his statue, known locally as 'the mannie'.

Walk up Fountain Road past the fountain and cross the street to go under the railway bridge, following the 'Ben Bhraggie' signposts. Bear right at Rhives Farm, before turning left up a signposted path to a gate.

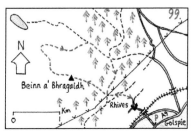

The path is well signposted as it ascends through woodland, crossing several forestry tracks. The whole area has seen a recent explosion in mountain bike trails and you should be vigilant regarding fast and furious downhill racers.

On reaching a line of pylons, the path follows them left for 100m before emerging on a wide forest road. Go right here for a few metres before rejoining the forest on the far side by a series of stone steps. After crossing another forest track higher up, continue steeply uphill to a complex wooden structure supporting a series

Beinn a'Bhragaidh from Loch Fleet

of ramps, crossing the deer fence at the upper forest edge. This has been purely designed for mountain bikes, enabling them to cross the deer fence without 'breaking their flow'. Mere walkers can go under the structure and go through the fence by a gate.

By now, the imposing monument dominates the skyline, but there is still a good 10–15 minutes of steep ascent helped by several stone steps. The sheer size of the monument is only apparent when you reach its foot at the hill's summit. Built in 1834, it commemorates the first Duke of Sutherland, who famously oversaw some of the most despicable and brutal evictions in the Straths of Sutherland during the Highland Clearances.

Such are the feelings of animosity towards the Duke that a strong steel mesh has been constructed round the base of the monument to prevent wilful vandalism of the stonework. There will always be those who see the statue as a glorification of a greedy and cruel villain, and others who believe the monument should remain as a reminder of those grim times.

One thing has remained constant throughout the centuries – that of seeing wild land only in economic terms. Whether it be through the introduction of sheep, blanket forestry or wind farms, money is at the root.

Rather than return the same way, follow the track which heads north-west in a series of bends before looping round to the right to descend gradually towards the forest edge at a gate on the north side of the hill. On reaching the main forest road, you can turn right to reach the upward ascent path at the pylons in about 1km. This is the quickest option.

Alternatively, cross the forest track and follow the cycle trail which loops round in a wide arc, eventually reaching the ascent path above Rhives Farm.

Beinn a' Bhragaidh monument

100. CREAG AN AMALAIDH (261M/856FT)

MAP	OS SHEET 21 (GR 759975)
DISTANCE	5KM
ASCENT	270M
TIME	1.5–2.5 HRS
ACCESS	CATTLE GRID PARKING SPACE (GR 767978)
DIFFICULTY	FAIRLY GOOD APPROACH AND RETURN TRACKS; EASY, GRASSY, PATHLESS ASCENT
SUMMARY	This conspicuous, craggy eminence rises high above Loch Fleet and is the finest of a handful of prominent little knolls in the immediate vicinity.

THE MEANING OF 'Amalaidh' is uncertain – '*amaladh*' is Gaelic for 'hindrance' and '*amarlaid*' is a 'blustering female'. 'Creag' is a reference to the significant band of conglomerate cliffs which adorn much of the eastern flank. The cairn on the summit is called Princess Cairn and possibly refers to a Norwegian princess who married a Skelbo Castle King in the 14th century.

The described circular route begins on the minor road which leaves the A9 just south of the Mound causeway.

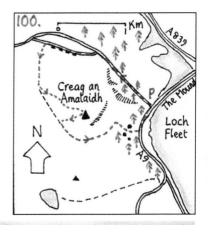

Creag an Amalaidh from Loch Fleet

View north from Creag an Amalaidh

There is a cattle grid and a small parking area on the right.

Walk up the minor road under a canopy of trees and take the left fork to Little Torboll, passing several stone cottages. After the last house on the left, turn left along a track going through a wooded area and a couple of gates. Cross a field to a third gate and emerge on open hillside.

Follow an old dry stone wall which heads directly up the heather slopes of the hill's western flank. Reach the hill's flat summit area and continue southwards to the small cairn perched above a line of crags.

As expected, the view is quite stunning, particularly eastward across the sea and sands of Loch Fleet, and round to the finger of the Portmahomack peninsula and Tarbat Ness.

Descend eastwards to reach the vehicle track which runs round the southern side of the hill. Turn left along the track, passing some stone circles and a massive, flattened cairn on the left-hand side, both signs of Bronze Age workings. Further on, pass a memorial on the left, before descending pleasantly through the wooded grounds of Cambusmore Estate. Pass the main house on the left and turn right through the Stables to reach the A9. Turn left and walk for 0.5km to reach the minor road and your starting point.

Index of Hill Names

(Hills marked * are not Marilyns)

Some other books published by **Luath Press**

Skye 360: Walking the Coastline of Skye
Andrew Dempster
ISBN: 978-1-910745-05-2 PBK £7.99

- 8 detailed maps and travel information
- Long-distance walks to day-trips
- Colour photographs
- Black and white sketches

One long walk divided into lots of short walks taking you all the way round Skye's rugged coastline.

Skye's plethora of peninsulas and sea-lochs contain awesome cliffs, remote beaches, storm tossed sea-stacks, natural arches, ancient duns, romantic castles, poignant Clearance settlements, tidal islands and idyllic secluded corners.

If you want to experience Skye in all its fascinating wealth of popular tourist haunts and hidden treasures, then let this book take you on a continuous 360-mile coastal walk around this mythical black island. You will soon find that there is a lot more to discover than the celebrated Cuillin ridge, mecca for walkers and climbers from all over the world.

Skye 360 is the perfect guidebook or whether you have a week, a weekend or just want to spend a day exploring a smaller part of the island.

Baffies' Easy Munro Guide
Volume 1: Southern Highlands
ISBN 978-1-908373-08-3 PBK £7.99
Volume 2: Central Highlands
ISBN 978-1-908373-20-5 PBK £7.99
Volume 3: The Cairngorms
ISBN 978-1-910745-05-2 PBK £7.99
Ralph Storer

Meet Baffies – the Entertainments Convenor of the Go-Take-A-Hike Mountaineering Club. Named after his footwear of choice ('Baffies' is a Scottish word for slippers), he's allergic to exertion, prone to lassitude, suffers from altitude sickness above 600m, blisters easily and bleeds readily. Show him a mountain and he'll find the easiest way up it. It's a gift of which he is justifiably proud and one whose fruits he has now been persuaded to share with like-minded souls. You'll find no easier way to climb Munros than to follow in his footsteps.

- Detailed descriptions of easy walking routes
- Annotated colour photographs and os maps
- Fascinating facts on landscape, history, Gaelic pronunciation

The perfect guidebooks to Scottish mountains for the hillwalker who wishes to avoid rock climbing, scrambling and vertigo.

Details of books published by Luath Press can be found at:
www.luath.co.uk

Luath Press Limited

committed to publishing well written books worth reading

LUATH PRESS takes its name from Robert Burns, whose little collie
Luath (*Gael.*, swift or nimble) tripped up Jean Armour at a wedding
and gave him the chance to speak to the woman who was to be his wife
and the abiding love of his life. Burns called one of the 'Twa Dogs'
Luath after Cuchullin's hunting dog in Ossian's *Fingal*.
Luath Press was established in 1981 in the heart of
Burns country, and is now based a few steps up
the road from Burns' first lodgings on
Edinburgh's Royal Mile. Luath offers you
distinctive writing with a hint of
unexpected pleasures.
Most bookshops in the UK, the US, Canada,
Australia, New Zealand and parts of Europe,
either carry our books in stock or can order them
for you. To order direct from us, please send a £sterling
cheque, postal order, international money order or your
credit card details (number, address of cardholder and
expiry date) to us at the address below. Please add post
and packing as follows: UK – £1.00 per delivery address;
overseas surface mail – £2.50 per delivery address; overseas airmail –
£3.50 for the first book to each delivery address, plus £1.00 for each
additional book by airmail to the same address. If your order is a gift,
we will happily enclose your card or message at no extra charge.

Luath Press Limited
543/2 Castlehill
The Royal Mile
Edinburgh EH1 2ND
Scotland
Telephone: +44 (0)131 225 4326 (24 hours)
Fax: +44 (0)131 225 4324
email: sales@luath. co.uk
Website: www. luath.co.uk